An Insider's Guide

GOLF'S GOLDEN COAST

ALGARVE
the complete course guide

Text by John Russell
Photos by Nuno Campos

VIP
VISTA IBÉRICA PUBLICAÇÕES

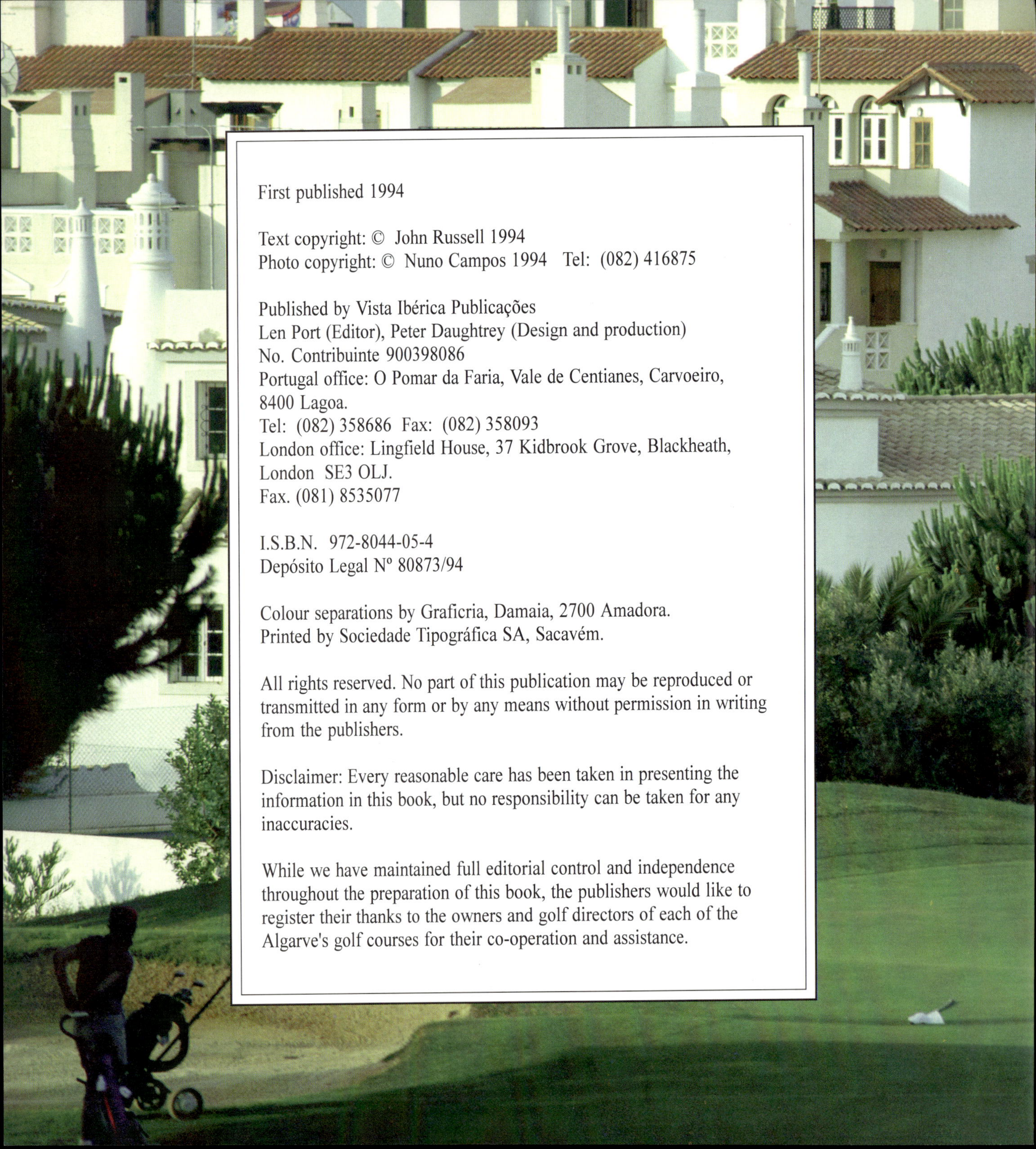

First published 1994

Published by Vista Ibérica Publicações
Len Port (Editor), Peter Daughtrey (Design and production)
No. Contribuinte 900398086
Portugal office: O Pomar da Faria, Vale de Centianes, Carvoeiro, 8400 Lagoa.
Tel: (082) 358686 Fax: (082) 358093
London office: Lingfield House, 37 Kidbrook Grove, Blackheath, London SE3 OLJ.
Fax. (081) 8535077

I.S.B.N. 972-8044-05-4
Depósito Legal Nº 80873/94

Colour separations by Graficria, Damaia, 2700 Amadora.
Printed by Sociedade Tipográfica SA, Sacavém.

While we have maintained full editorial control and independence throughout the preparation of this book, the publishers would like to register their thanks to the owners and golf directors of each of the Algarve's golf courses for their co-operation and assistance.

Contents

MONCHIQUE
SILVES
Penina
PORTIMAO
LAGOA
Quinta do Gramacho
Palmares
Alto Golf
Vale da Pinta
LAGOS
Parque da Floresta
Vale do Milho
Salgados
SAGRES

LOULÉ
Vilamoura I, II, III
Vila Sol
ALMANSIL
Vale do Lobo
Quinta do Lago
Pinheiros Altos
San Lorenzo
FARO
TAVIRA
VILA REAL DE
SANTO ANTÓNIO

FOREWORD

I have a very clear memory of my first visit to the Algarve. It was in 1981 when, as the new Editor of *Golf Monthly*, I was invited to visit what is now known as the Old Course at Vilamoura.

In those days it was simply Vilamoura, for this splendid layout was then the only golf course on the estate. I was greeted at the clubhouse by a tall, silver-haired gentleman with a soft and refined English accent who ruled his club with the precision and discipline of a Major-General.

David Green contributed greatly to the development of golf in the Algarve. He was then, and still is, one of the nicest people you will meet on a day's march. It was the start of a long and valued friendship. Sadly in this changing world David no longer parades and inspects the visitors to this beautiful golf course among the umbrella pines, but the memory of those glorious spring days, wonderful company and cool beer on the clubhouse patio will always linger.

I have returned time and time again to the Algarve and relish every visit. There are wonderful memories too of the late Sir Henry Cotton holding court at his beloved Penina and hours spent with him on the practice ground with his tyre and his insistence that my hands were better than my game. Alas, I fear, I remained a disappointment to the great man for I never did realise the ambition he optimistically held, that he could return me once more to category one from whence too long before I had departed.

But what marvellous fun there was in trying and what priceless knowledge was learned at the hands of one of the greatest players in the history of our game.

It was Henry Cotton who took golf to the Algarve in the late 1960's when he realised his vision of building a classic test of golf alongside one of the great hotels in continental Europe. Where the great man led many were to follow and today there is set before the visitor a veritable feast of golfing pleasure from the beautiful Quinta do Lago estate close to the international airport at Faro in the east, to the glories of Palmares, with its stretch of classic links golf in the west, and today even beyond that.

In this excellent, well-illustrated book, John Russell and Nuno Campos set out the complete guide to golf in the Algarve with all the information the visitor will need to enjoy one of the game's finest and most beautiful destinations.

It is concise, informative, interesting and attractive. Reading it has brought back many happy memories and I commend it to you.

Malcolm L. Campbell
Travel Editor, *Golf Monthly*

Introduction

The Algarve, a mere two to three hours flight from most European capitals, has been a magnet to many discerning golfers for almost three decades.

Portugal's southernmost province is justly famous for its spectacular scenery along a fabulous coastline highlighted by honey-coloured cliffs protecting coves and bays and sandy strands washed clean by the translucent Atlantic Ocean.

Add to this 14 beautifully tended golf complexes, a friendly climate, a cosmopolitan culture and wholesome regional cooking, all in a compact area steeped in history, and you have the ultimate in year-round golfing destinations.

Portugal's golf history is one of the oldest on mainland Europe - providing, of course, one disregards the ancient origins of such games as *kolven* which the Dutch indulged in, and the rudimentary sport of *paganica* which the Romans played with enthusiasm.

Golf in Portugal completed its centenary in 1990. The first course was originally called the St. Skeff Links - now the Oporto Golf Club - near the seaside town of Espinho, south of Oporto. This was only the fourth golf course to be built on the Continent, after those at Pau, Antwerp's Royal Club and Biarritz.

The first course in the Algarve was a small, rudimentary layout built in the 1920's between Portimão and the nearby beach of Praia da Rocha. Because of a lack of freshwater, its "greens" were "browns" and consisted of a mixture of sand and oil. A few hardy addicts played on this course for little more than a decade before it became extinct.

It was the legendary Henry Cotton who put the Algarve on the golf map. In the mid-sixties at Penina he designed the first proper grass course. It was the first of three he designed in the Algarve, a place he loved and made his home for almost 30 years.

During the 1970's the 1980's and on into the first half of the 1990's, golf courses mushroomed all along Portugal's south coast as it became increasingly attractive to holidaymakers from northern Europe. Golf is now played at seventeen distinct courses with a total of 342 widely differing holes.

Strangely enough, all the existing courses lie west of the regional capital, Faro, although a few projects have been mooted for the eastern Algarve between Faro and the Spanish border.

None of the existing courses is more than 15 km from the coast. Yet the terrain varies from the steep hillsides of Parque da Floresta to the near sea-level flatlands of Vilamoura III and the most recently opened course at Salgados which, in common with Palmares, includes links holes. The terrain typical of most courses, however, gently undulates through copses of attractive umbrella pines.

The mainly arid Algarve countryside familiar to summer visitors gives way to verdant oases at each of the fourteen golf complexes thanks to large, state-funded water catchment and distribution schemes, as well as private boreholes which tap into subterranean water sources for irrigation. Holes made tricky by water hazards are, therefore, not an infrequent feature on Algarve courses.

So many courses have been opened in the Algarve during the past few years that golfers, even if they know the region fairly well, may not be acquainted with all of them. Hopefully, this guide will be of practical help to those who want to bring themselves up-to-date with the latest developments in the Algarve golfing scene.

Future editions of the book will include any new courses which open. Although many have been talked about or planned over the past decade in an attempt to cash in on the European golf boom, not many are actually in the pipeline. Only three seem to be still active in the planning stage at present: at Quinta Benamor near Tavira, Castro Marim beside the Guadiana river which separates the Algarve from Spanish Andalusia, and near the historic town of Silves.

Golf is an all-year-round sport in the Algarve, though the main season is from late autumn to late spring. Winters are mild and golfers from northern European countries can enjoy warm, sunny days and keep their swings smooth at a time when their home courses are unplayable.

Be warned, however, that despite southern Portugal's appealing sunshine statistics, rain does fall from time to time and nearly all of it during the main golfing season. Furthermore, the thermometer occasionally, just occasionally, drops towards freezing point in the early morning in winter. Come prepared for the worst with warm clothing and waterproofs.

The problem in summer may be keeping cool. Strict dress codes are enforced at most clubs and this means that shorts must be of the tailored type and men's shirts must not be sleeveless. Note also that the wearing of jeans in any season is prohibited at nearly all clubs.

By visiting during the main golf season you avoid the crowded roads and added accommodation costs that come with the summer tourist trade. On the other hand, during the summer months all of the courses are under utilised, so more leisurely, relaxing rounds can be enjoyed.

Specialist travel agencies offer a range of golfing packages, but visitors who are interested in more variety and flexibility have several other options. Many of the courses offer multiple green fee tickets at varying discounts for limited periods. During the warmer months, take advantage of the reduced green fees available at several courses for midday and/or evening teeing off times.

The local regional golf association, Algarve Golfe, has introduced a "passport" which can be purchased at several golf clubs offering reduced green fees at selected courses. The current (late 1994) price of this practical and economical "passport," valid for five 18-hole rounds, is 30,000$ (about £125). Courses participating in the scheme are: Quinta do Lago, Pinheiros Altos, Vale do Lobo, Vilamoura, Vila Sol, Pine Cliffs, Penina and Palmares. The reception offices at these courses will be happy to supply full information upon request.

Visiting golfers will also find that they are welcome to play at a reasonable cost in most of the many local tournaments. It is well worth finding out about up-coming tournaments from the various clubs before or as soon as you arrive.

On a technical note, the lengths given for the courses and individual holes are from the championship tees, and if you play from the forward tees you will need to check the distances from the score cards. If you are more accustomed to yards, don't forget that adding 10 per cent to the lengths in metres will provide the approximate yard-ages.

Although golf is easily the main sport played in the Algarve by visitors and residents alike, plenty of other sports activities can be enjoyed throughout the year. They include tennis, squash, horse-riding, clay-pigeon shooting, micro-light flying and the whole gamut of water sports

from surfing to scuba-diving.

Not all the best or the most popular restaurants and bars frequented by summer visitors remain open throughout the October to April golf season, but there is always a good choice of eating and drinking establishments which do not close.

Winter and spring visitors interested in natural history have the opportunity of observing a wide variety of plant and bird life in the Ria Formosa and other protected areas while hoping for another type of birdie on nearby greens.

In general, you will find that the Algarve, with its mild climate, reasonably priced restaurants, breathtaking scenery, friendly people and excellent golf courses, all combine to make it a memorable holiday.

SAN LORENZO

Pages 12-13:
The legendary 18th

Opposite page:
A typically well-defended green

Right:
Peninsular 18th green

Below:
The beguiling 8th hole

Exclusive, immaculate - a natural showpiece

Although open since 1988 only, San Lorenzo has built up an enviable reputation as a course you must play if you are in the Algarve. Exclusivity obviously plays a part, but the sheer magnificence of San Lorenzo and its rating among the top three courses in Europe prove that attention to detail and meticulous maintenance make it the show-piece of the region.

British comedian Jimmy Tarbuck has regularly held his Golf Classic here, bringing sports personalities and show business celebrities from the United Kingdom, such as Henry Cooper, Jasper Carrott, Tim Brooke-Taylor, plus many more who have all returned year after year.

A leading pro brings the British Daily Telegraph Junior Golf Championship finals each year to San Lorenzo. This prestigious event is generously supported by local attendance and Forte Hotels.

Perhaps the most attractive element associated with this course is the way in which it blends into the natural environment of the area. Of several courses in the region, it shares the splendid setting and beauty of the Ria Formosa Nature Reserve. Flora and fauna are exquisite, making the course a delight to both golfer and casual visitor.

In general terms San Lorenzo is regarded as a players' course with a sensible approach rather than spectacular chances. It is the variety of the holes that makes the course particularly attractive.

The five opening holes are on typical Algarve golf terrain, undulating and with the omnipresent pinetrees, although they do not encroach unduly on to the fairways.

After the climb to the green of the pleasant 129-metre fifth you are able to

Above: 9th green and clubhouse

Left: Driving range

Looking across from 18th fairway to the 8th

glimpse the sea with its sandbars not far offshore and the wonderful overall view of the coastline to the east. Since the tricky sixth and seventh hug this coastline, golfers need to keep their concentration and not deviate from the narrow fairways.

Not surprisingly, the sixth is stroke index 1, a par 4 from a raised tee with a fairway which dog-legs left. Most golfers play safe off the tee, but by thus leaving a longer approach to the small green tucked in close to the water's edge, scoring par becomes somewhat more difficult.

After the similar seventh, but with a straight fairway, the tough 525-metre par 5 eighth is a hole to be remembered. It cuts inland, but a large fresh water lake on the right affects play from tee to green, the latter perilously placed on a promontory.

The back nine also has some excellent holes, including the 473-metre long fifteenth where bunker-dodging on the normal three shots to the green is the main objective.

But San Lorenzo is famous for the two exciting finishing holes. Both are average length par 4's where you must try to stay out of the lakes and bunkers at all cost to avoid ruining your scorecard. On the seventeenth the water threatens on the left both for tee-shot and approach.

The final hole is one of the legendary holes in the Algarve to write home about. A well placed drive out to the right is needed to steer away from the lake. Then there is not much of an escape route to an almost island green guarded by three bunkers. So a courageous approach is practically the only option. Who can ever forget such a formidable final hole?

Opposite page: Short 14th bending on to par 5 15th

COURSE INFORMATION

OWNED BY: *Forte Hotels,*
Hotel Dona Filipa,
Vale do Lobo,
8135 Almancil.
Tel: (089) 396522, 396534
Fax: (089) 396908
Telex: 56848

GOLF DIRECTOR: *António Santos*
PRO: *Albano Rodrigues*

COURSE DESIGNER: *Joseph Lee (on site)*
ARCHITECT: *William Roquemore*

FOUNDED: *1988*

NO. OF HOLES: *18. Par (SSS): 72 (73)*

LENGTH IN METRES: *6,238*

LAST IMPORTANT TOURNAMENT: *Daily Telegraph Juniors Championship - Finals; Jimmy Tarbuck Golf Classic 1994.*

GREEN FEES: *Free to clients of Dona Filipa and Penina Hotels*
Visitors: 18 holes -12,500$
9 holes - 7,500$

REQUIREMENTS TO PLAY AS A VISITOR:
Handicap certificates - Max. 28 men;
36 ladies.
Strict dress code enforced. Starting times bookable maximum 24 hours in advance for visitors.

AMENITIES

Pro shop
Driving range: access fee - 500$
70 balls - 1,500$
Putting-green
Chipping green
Academy
Lessons: (clinics - 4 to 10 persons)
1 hour - 3,500$ per player
2 hours - 5,000$ per player
(11 to 20 persons)
1 hour - 2,500$ per player
2 hours - 3,500$ per player
Club hire: 4,000$
Trolleys: 750$
Powakaddy: 2,500$
Buggies: 18 holes - 7,500$; 9 holes - 5,500$

CLUBHOUSE:
Traditional wooden construction, central entrance with facilities office, pro shop, showers, lockers, etc. Restaurant for lunch and bar snacks.

CATERING: *Bar, Restaurant and snacks*
On course: Bar and snacks buggy

OTHER ATTRACTIONS

Quinta do Lago *estate facilities - including good restaurants and two nature trails.*
Ria Formosa Nature Reserve - *many species of wading birds and waterfowl.*
Beach - *Quinta do Lago beach is the nearest.*
Horse-riding centres - *three in the area.*
Faro - *museums and shopping.*

HOW TO FIND: *Twenty kms from Faro Airport on the Quinta do Lago estate, south of the village of Almancil which is just off the EN125 main road running roughly parallel to the coast. The way to Quinta do Lago is well-signposted from Almancil.*

> *❛Recently regraded up from 8th to 3rd in the listing of Europe's finest golf courses behind Valderrama and El Saler.❜*
>
> Andrew White,
> Former Director of Golf, Forte Hotels Portugal.

MENS S.S.S. 73										LADIES S.S.S. 73		
HOLE	WHITE	YELLOW	PAR	S.I.			WON LOST POINTS			RED	PAR	S.I.
1	494	473	5	7						440	5	7
2	162	133	3	15						111	3	15
3	334	296	4	13						257	4	13
4	339	318	4	5						289	4	5
5	129	108	3	17						96	3	17
6	386	365	4	1						298	4	1
7	345	328	4	11						299	4	11
8	525	495	5	3						465	5	3
9	366	352	4	9						312	4	9
OUT	3080	2868	36							2567	36	
DISTANCE IN METRES										DISTANCE IN METRES		
10	519	492	5	12						385	5	12
11	350	336	4	14						280	4	14
12	395	368	4	2						349	4	2
13	359	337	4	8						308	4	8
14	157	143	3	18						133	3	18
15	473	455	5	6						405	5	6
16	190	172	3	16						121	3	16
17	344	317	4	10						296	4	10
18	371	349	4	4						327	4	4
IN	3158	2969	36							2604	36	
OUT	3080	2868	36							2567	36	
TOTAL	6238	5837	72							5171	72	
	HANDICAP											
	RESULT											

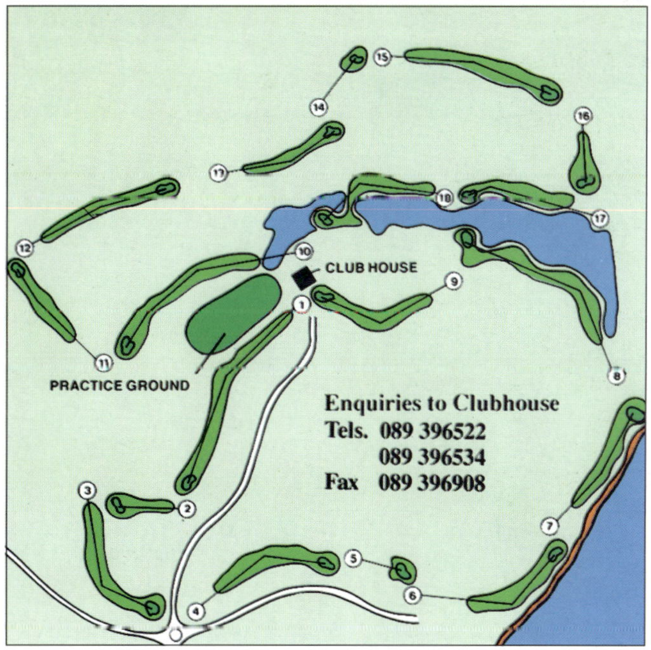

Pinheiros Altos

Accurate shooting needed next to nature reserve

Pinheiros Altos, located within the exclusive Quinta do Lago estate, benefits from the adjoining Ria Formosa Nature Reserve. Bird life and exotic plants abound and this golf course displays them wonderfully.

There are distinctly different halves at Pinheiros Altos: the first nine holes are in an undulating, pine covered landscape; the second nine are in a contrasting lakeside setting. Accuracy is paramount on this championship golf course. This is amply emphasised on the opening hole.

The first drive is straightforward to a wide landing area, but with a dog-leg second shot to a green protected by tall pine

Above: Egrets feeding near 16th green

Left: Short 17th

Pages 22-3: The short 5th

Right: 2nd green

trees. Already the player will be aware of the intricacies and subtle hazards presented by the course designer.

The par 3 second is 168 metres long and requires precision since any wayward shot is heavily punished - thrown away from the green if left, or bunkered front and right.

Hole number five has all the makings of becoming a world famous par 3. From a raised tee to an elevated green and with a carry of some 143 metres, it is an awesome hole. Wind, humidity and nerves all come into play, especially when one sees the valley filled with pine trees, a steeply sloping green and a huge, dominating pine looming over the left corner of the green. On the second nine, hole number

Below: Well defended 18th

twelve, a par 4, represents a true test of ability and character. A positive drive to a narrowing fairway with a lake to the left requires both precision and fearlessness. The second shot to the small, water-fronted green very often results in humility. A strong dose of accuracy and courage reward the player handsomely.

The short par 3 seventeenth, an innocent shot over water to a substantial green, is really a "wolf in sheep's clothing". The green is severely stepped and anything other than a solidly struck and well placed tee shot is punished.

Deservedly, Pinheiros Altos has a strong following of golfers from all parts of Europe. The course represents variety and interest, but visitors also praise the enthusiasm of service and attention given by all the staff associated with Pinheiros Altos.

Opposite page: 11th green

Left: 7th hole through trees

Below: Practice facilities in front of 1st fairway

COURSE INFORMATION

OWNED BY:
London & Edinburgh Trust P.L.C.,
Quinta do Lago,
8135 Almancil.
Tel: (089) 394340
Fax: (089) 394392

GOLF DIRECTOR: *Wayne Johnson*
PRO: *Steve Simpkin*

COURSE ARCHITECT: *Ronald Fream*

FOUNDED: *1992*

Nº. OF HOLES: *18. Par (SSS): 71 (72)*

LENGTH IN METRES: *6,057*

LAST IMPORTANT TOURNAMENTS:
Johnnie Walker Euro Classic;
Glenfiddich Pro-Am
T.A.P. Pro-Am Series;
Golfreisen and numerous
PGA Pro-Ams throughout the year.

GREEN FEES: *(For 1994/5 season)*
18 holes - 9,000$, inclusive of "Strokesaver"
9 holes - 5,000$
5-day ticket - 40,000$

REQUIREMENTS TO PLAY AS A VISITOR:
Handicap certificates - max. 28 men, 36 ladies. Strict dress code, i.e. collared shirts and tailored shorts.

AMENITIES

Pro shop		
Driving range	*50 balls*	*700$*
Putting-greens (3)		
Chipping green and practice bunker		
Academy		
Lessons	*1/2 hour*	*4.000$*
Club hire		
Trolleys	*18 holes*	*800$*
	9 holes	*500$*
Buggies	*18 holes*	*7.000$*
	9 holes	*4.000$*
Caddies by request		
Locker room facilities		

CLUBHOUSE: *Probably the most pleasant on the Algarve; variety of bars, restaurants, showers, locker rooms, sauna and lounges.*

CATERING: *bars, snack bar and restaurant in the clubhouse. On course: Roving buggy with drinks and snacks.*

OTHER ATTRACTIONS

Quinta do Lago - *estate facilities, including good restaurants and two nature trails;*
Ria Formosa Nature Park;
Beach - *at Quinta do Lago;*
Horse-riding centres - *three in the area;*
Faro - *museums and shopping.*

HOW TO FIND: *20 kms west of Faro airport on the Quinta do Lago estate. There are three main roads to the coast from the village of Almancil. The one farthest to the east leads to the course and the route is well signposted.*

A course of great contrast providing a comprehensive range of challenges.

Peter McEvoy, former world amateur champion and Walker Cup team player.

The mature Pinheiros Altos golf course can offer memorable, dramatic, unique playing enjoyment to golfers of all levels of ability.

Ronald Fream, course architect.

The Pines										
CHAMPIONSHIP	365	194	313	329	159	542	429	515	371	3217
MEDAL	338	168	288	300	143	522	386	483	356	2984
REGULAR	306	133	227	280	142	500	355	454	316	2713
STROKE INDEX	13	17	1	3	11	9	5	7	15	
PAR	4	3	4	4	3	5	4	5	4	36
HOLE	1	2	3	4	5	6	7	8	9	OUT
PAR	4	3	4	4	3	5	4	5	4	36
STROKE INDEX	13	17	1	3	11	9	5	7	15	
LADIES	279	108	211	257	131	474	330	430	296	2516

The Lakes											
CHAMPIONSHIP	325	385	330	541	201	303	304	113	338	2840	6057
MEDAL	304	353	303	519	186	279	290	98	298	2630	5614
REGULAR	287	345	281	490	143	251	266	91	278	2432	5145
STROKE INDEX	14	2	8	6	12	4	10	18	16		
PAR	4	4	4	5	3	4	4	3	4	35	71
HOLE	10	11	12	13	14	15	16	17	18	IN	TOTAL
PAR	4	4	4	5	3	4	4	3	4	35	71
STROKE INDEX	14	2	8	6	12	4	10	18	16		
LADIES	270	319	253	440	130	241	256	81	256	2246	4762

Standard scratch score ● 72 ○ 70 ● 69 ● 72

Quinta do Lago

Challenging choices for all levels of play

Above: Right-hand side view of 15th on new TPC course

Pages 32-33: Back view of same hole

Quinta do Lago is probably the best known of the Algarve's golf courses, primarily because it has hosted the Portuguese Open seven times. The B and C 9-hole loops, combined in January 1995 to form the TPC championship course, are a delightful experience for players of all standards. The 1989 Open here was the first Volvo Tour event won by Colin Montgomerie. He scored 24 under par and established a new course record of 63.

The holes meander through the spectacular 2,000-acre Quinta do Lago estate created in 1973 to provide exclusive residential and recreational facilities. The Ria Formosa Nature Reserve, a 45,500-acre protected area, has part of its boundaries within the estate. It is one of the last

Right: TPC 1st green seen from the rough

Above: TPC 16th hole looking towards the Ria Formosa reserve

unspoilt coastal zones in Europe. The terrain is gently undulating and features several lakes.

Both the TPC and the Ria Formosa (formerly A + D) courses provide a solid test for players of all levels of ability - the sign of any great golf course. With 36 holes to choose from, it becomes a little difficult to narrow down to the exceptional ones at Quinta do Lago. Perhaps the most memorable and obvious hole is the 200-metre par 3 fifteenth on the TPC course with its scenic lake, long wooden bridge and large green set in amongst the trees. In Fernando Nunes Pedro's book, *Golf in Portugal*, where a panel of local experts selected holes from Portuguese courses to form their "dream" course, this hole was a unanimous

Below: TPC 15th hole with 14th on left and 17th top right of photo

choice. Short hitters may find the long carry over the lake somewhat daunting, but any golfer who puts his tee-shot on the green here can experience a real sense of achievement.

On the first nine of the TPC course, there are several fine holes, the double dog-leg 505-metre fifth being the better of the two testing par 5's. You must thread your

drive between the bunkers on either side of the sloping fairway at about the 220-metre mark. Then the large pine trees high on the left tend to make you steer your second shot to the right where more trees lurk further ahead. The elevated green is well defended by bunkers front and right, and a large pine on the left.

Another tricky raised green can be encountered on the dog-leg right par 4 eighth. To set up the ideal approach shot, a long drive with a fade is desirable to counteract the severe right to left sloping fairway as it emerges from the trees on the right. The awkwardly sloping green is cut into a steep bank, so it is preferable to execute a high approach with enough carry to pitch on to the putting surface.

The tough par 4 tenth hole, which used to open the C course, is 410 metres in length and worthy of special mention. A longish drive is desirable, but the bunker on the left and trees on the right are ready to catch anything off line. The distance of the approach shot over a large dip to the large sloping green is deceptive, so club selection is critical.

On the newly designated Ria Formosa course (ex A + D loops) there is an abundance of dog-legged par 4's and 5's. The relatively short par 4 tenth (358 metres) has a fairly generous fairway although it falls away a little to the left. But the secret here is judging the approach to the subtly undulating green since it needs a deft touch. With bunkers at the front and left and a bank on the right, it is not infrequent to see shots roll through into a hidden bunker guarding

the back of the green.

The twelfth is also an excellent short par 4 measuring 361 metres, but it is almost always essential to cut across the 90 degree dog-leg left over a large lake, shortening the distance considerably. There is not much point in going for length off the tee - just play it safe. In fact, a leading Scottish amateur girl golfer was asked her opinion of this hole a couple of years ago. The answer was: "Nae bother. Seeven iron aff the tee, and an easy five wood tae the green".

The eigtheenth is an excellent test of golf with plenty of variety. The drive requires a long carry over a lake to a fairway sloping right to left at the landing area, luring shots to the left hand bunkers. The tree-lined fairway veers to the right and dips down for the second shot, rising again for the approach towards a slick double-tiered green. This is a monumental finishing hole

Above: Long par 5 TPC 12th

Left: Green flanking Lakeside Village

Page 38 top: Clubhouse overlooking 1st fairway

Page 38 bottom: 17th TPC tee and 16th green

Page 39: Lengthy summer evening shadows

3rd TPC green

for the Ria Formosa course.

Apart from its well publicised association with the Portuguese Open and a history of being a forerunner in golf promotion, Quinta do Lago also has a much lighter side. For instance Spanish couple Alberto Rodriguez and Concepcion Payno, golfing fanatics, invited Golf Director Mário Barruncho as godfather to the christening of their son Alberto. Not an unusual occurrence in itself, but the location of the ceremony was the lake adjacent to the fifteenth hole on the TPC course.

Also, a couple of years ago a local architect, José Madeira, drove off on the seventeenth hole of the same course. It was not exactly an exemplary drive golf-wise, but the ball whistled low and with great velocity across the lake, striking a fish which had leapt out of the water. José unfortunately lost his ball and the hole, but nevertheless gained a substantial aquatic trophy.

Above: Gracious greenside living

Left: Clubhouse

COURSE INFORMATION

OWNED BY: *PLANAL, S.A.,*
Soc. do Golfe da Quinta do Lago S.A.,
Quinta do Lago,
8135 Almancil.
Tel: (089) 396002/3
Fax: (089) 394013

GOLF DIRECTOR: *Mário Barruncho*
GOLF SECRETARY: *José António Capela*
PRO'S: *Domingos Silva, Rogério Valente and Sebastião Gil*

COURSE ARCHITECT:
A, B and C 9-hole loops - William Mitchell.
D 9-hole loop - Joseph Lee, Designer;
William Roquemore, Architect

FOUNDED: *A & B - 1974;*
C - 1975; D - 1991

Nº. OF HOLES: *36.*
Par (SSS): TPC course (old B+C) 72 (74);
Ria Formosa course (old A+D) 72 (72);

LENGTH IN METRES: *Average 6,350*

LAST IMPORTANT TOURNAMENTS:
Portuguese Open (seven times, last in 1990);
Johnnie Walker Euro Classic, 1994.

GREEN FEES: *(from 1st October 1994 until 30th September 1995)*
18 holes - 11,000$
18 holes (members' guests and members of Portuguese Clubs) - 5,500$
18 holes (residents, owners Clube da Quinta, Four Seasons, Vilar do Golf, Victory Village, Bovis, Quinta do Lago Hotel, Four Seasons Fairways) - 8,000$
18 holes (tour operators)
(1/10/94 - 30/4/95) - 8,500$
(1/5/95 - 30/9/95) - 7,500$
9 holes - 50% discount

REQUIREMENTS TO PLAY AS A VISITOR: *Current handicap certificate. (Those without may have a competence test with a professional at Quinta do Lago.).*

AMENITIES

Pro shop
Driving range: 500$
Ball machine: 50 balls - 600$
Putting-green
Chipping green
Academy
Boutique
Lessons: 1/2 hour - 4,000$
Club hire:
18 holes - 4,000$
9 holes - 2,500$
Trolleys: 750$
Buggies:
18 holes - 7,000$
9 holes - 4,000$

HOW TO FIND: *Quinta do Lago estate is 3 kms south of the village of Almancil which is just off the EN 125 main road running roughly parallel to the coast. The way to Quinta do Lago is well signposted.*

Caddie:
18 holes - 4,000$
9 holes - 2,500$

(These prices are subject to revision)

CLUBHOUSE: *Spacious split level building with terrace bar and snack facility overlooking the first tee of the B course. The lounge/ restaurant serves as a meeting place as well. The Clube de Golfe da Quinta do Lago have their own private lounge within the clubhouse which also serves as a meeting and presentation area. An extensive locker room area and reception take up the lower floor of the complex.*

CATERING: *Clubhouse - Bar and Restaurant facilities. On courses - Small snack bars at various points. Larger bar and snack facility beside first tee on D course.*

TPC course																					
CHAMP	390	500	387	171	505	350	182	385	355	3225	410	190	460	325	383	200	372	510	413	3263	6488
MEN	345	470	350	135	480	315	160	350	320	2925	375	160	425	285	350	160	330	490	370	2945	5870
LADIES	320	415	285	110	435	290	142	320	290	2607	340	112	380	255	300	125	270	465	338	2585	5192
PAR	4	5	4	3	5	4	3	4	4	36	4	3	5	4	4	3	4	5	4	36	72
BURACO HOLE	1	2	3	4	5	6	7	8	9	OUT	10	11	12	13	14	15	16	17	18	IN	Total
STROKE INDEX	11	3	7	17	1	13	15	5	9		2	18	8	12	10	14	16	4	6		

Ria Formosa course																					
CHAMP	367	180	510	380	345	319	504	153	380	3138	358	465	361	374	154	370	160	345	480	3067	6205
MEN	340	145	480	350	320	307	484	140	367	2933	349	450	348	358	141	335	130	320	440	2871	5804
LADIES	300	110	435	330	310	268	368	111	326	2558	326	412	238	328	114	310	95	265	385	2473	5031
PAR	4	3	5	4	4	4	5	3	4	36	4	5	4	4	3	4	3	4	5	36	72
BURACO HOLE	1	2	3	4	5	6	7	8	9	OUT	10	11	12	13	14	15	16	17	18	IN	Total
STROKE INDEX	11	17	1	7	9	13	3	15	5		12	4	6	10	16	8	18	14	2		

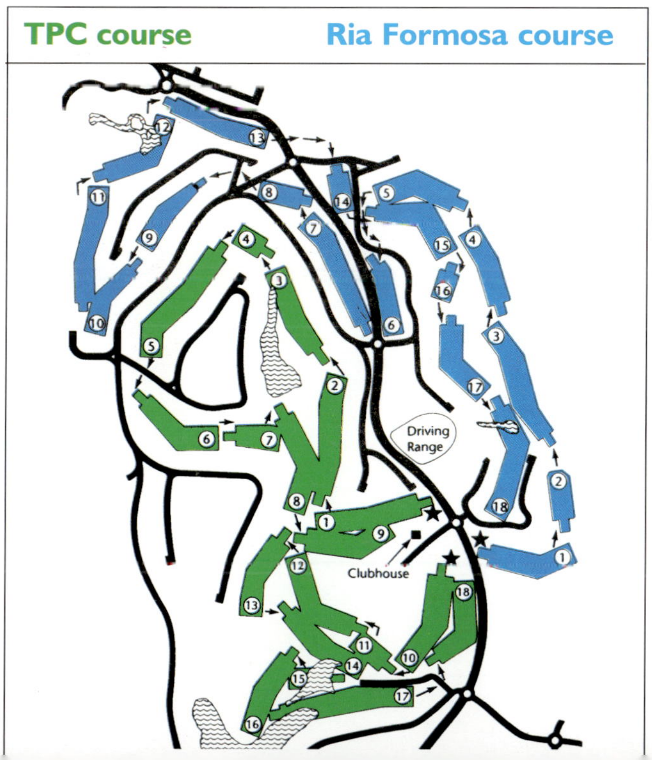

OTHER ATTRACTIONS

Quinta do Lago *- all the facilities of this five-star resort.*
Ria Formosa Nature Reserve *with its varied flora and fauna.*
Beach *at Quinta do Lago.*
Horse-riding centres *- three in the area.*
Faro *- museums and shopping.*

> " Quinta do Lago is a worthy example of golfing quality and excellence being provided without endangering the natural beauty of the area. It really is a place in a million. "
>
> Renton Ladlaw, golf writer and broadcaster.

VALE DO LOBO

Pages 46-9:
The famous 7th on Yellow course

Narrow-mindedness is a virtue - except at the seventh

Vale do Lobo initially developed quite slowly. The first two nines (Yellow and Orange courses) were officially opened in 1968, the following nine (Green) not until 1974. A further nine holes, already designed by Sir Henry Cotton, are still awaiting completion.

The Yellow course opens with a comfortable 428 metres par 5. Thereafter, narrow fairways and well protected greens make scoring par difficult at times. The greens overall are tricky since many have severe run-offs due to their elevated positions.

Accuracy becomes the watchword at the impressive seventh hole. At 210 metres over two ravines, it's practically all carry. With the tee located on the clifftop affording spectacular views, overcoming the wind and nerves plays a major part in making a successful tee-shot to the green of this hole.

Much like the Yellow, the Orange course disguises its challenge with subtle use of narrow fairways and protected greens. The first hole requires precision off the tee and common sense for the second shot. A stream crosses the fairway, well in front of the green, inviting a long carry or a short iron to set up the approach to the green.

Right: Orange course, 7th green on left, 2nd hole on right

The very tricky sixth hole runs alongside the beach. A 178-metre par 3 may seem comfortable, but on-shore breezes and a full carry demand concentration.

The Green course continues the confined fairway feel of the other two and adds a further dimension. Meandering narrow fairways demand good placing and any wayward shot is heavily penalised. None illustrates this better than the par 5 fourth. The drive is to a narrow landing zone between trees, and then you need either an immense second shot over a copse, or a short iron to the opening of the dog-leg with a subsequent punch shot into the green.

Vale do Lobo is also distinguished by its attraction to personalities from all over Europe. Among the many who enjoy the

Below: Orange course overview

facilities offered are former German soccer star, Franz Beckenbauer, and the BBC's Judith Chalmers with husband Neil Durden-Smith. Miss Chalmers has recently been awarded an O.B.E. in recognition of her contribution to the tourist industry.

The intention is to replace the existing combination of three nine hole courses with two 18-hole courses. The existing Orange course will combine with the Green, and a new nine will be added to the Yellow.

Above:
1st green approach, Orange course

Left: Typical Vale do Lobo terrain

Holes-in-one these days are still relatively difficult to attain, but Vale do Lobo has an interesting anecdote to recount on the subject. A four-ball, including two residents of the complex, were playing a 'friendly' round on the par 3 fourth hole of the Orange course. Mike Borissow, a 10 handicapper, struck a seven wood shot straight into the hole; his opponent David Carter, who plays off five, repeated the performance with a seven iron - also straight into the cup. No-one has related the comments expressed between the 'friendly' foursome. No doubt, however, it was exceedingly expensive.

Opposite page: 1st tee on Green course

Left: 5th hole on Yellow course

Below: 5th on Orange course. The Front Cover depicts the other end of this hole.

COURSE INFORMATION

OWNED BY: *Vale do Lobo, Lda.,*
8137 Vale do Lobo Codex,
Tel: (089) 393939. Fax: (089) 394713

GOLF DIRECTOR: *Mrs. Janet Walker*
PRO: *Stephen Walker*

COURSE ARCHITECT: *Sir Henry Cotton*

FOUNDED: *1968*

NO. OF HOLES: *27.*
Par (SSS): Yellow/Orange 72 (73)
Orange/Green 71 (71) - Green/Yellow 71 (71)

LENGTH IN METRES: *Yellow/Orange 5,909; Orange/Green 5,448; Green/Yellow 5,649*

LAST IMPORTANT TOURNAMENTS: *Open Foursomes Europe's Finest 1st Amateur Week; Johnnie Walker Euro Classic.*

GREEN FEES:

	Visitors	*Welcome card*	*Guest card*	*Club card*
Daily	*10,000$*	*7,500$*	*5,000$*	*2,500$*
Weekly	*--$*	*--$*	*25,000$*	*12,500$*
Fortnightly	*--$*	*--$*	*40,000$*	*20,000$*
Monthly	*--$*	*--$*	*57,500$*	*--$*
Annual		*--$*	*--$*	*52,000$*
Annual - couple -				*93,500$*
Annual couple with Private buggy	*--$*	*--$*	*--$*	*100,000$*

REQUIREMENTS TO PLAY AS A VISITOR: *Handicap certificate requested. Strict dress code.*

AMENITIES

Pro shop
Driving range (Barringtons)
Putting-green
Chipping green
Academy

Lessons:	*4,000$*	*3,500$*	*3,250$*	*3,000$*
Club hire:	*6,000$*	*4,000$*	*3,000$*	*1,500$*
Trolleys:	*1,000$*	*750$*	*500$*	*250$*
Buggies:				
9 holes -	*8,000$*	*6,000$*	*3,500$*	*2,800$*
18 holes -	*11,000$*	*8,250$*	*5,500$*	*3,800$*

(Only Vale do Lobo buggies and Vale do Lobo annual Golf Club Members' buggies are permitted on the Golf Course)
Locker room facilities

CLUBHOUSE: *Bar, lounge and restaurant. Changing rooms and lockers adjacent. Terrace overlooking 1st tee Yellow course and putting green.*

CATERING: *Bar, snack bar, restaurant in the clubhouse.*
On the course: roving buggy with drinks and snacks.

OTHER ATTRACTIONS

Vale do Lobo - *comprehensive resort facilities, including beach bars and restaurants.*
Sports - *facilities include bowling, croquet, swimming pools and tennis centre.*

HOW TO FIND: *20 Kms west of Faro Airport and reached via the village of Almancil. Of the three main roads to the coast from Almancil, the one farthest to the west leads to the course which is well signposted.*

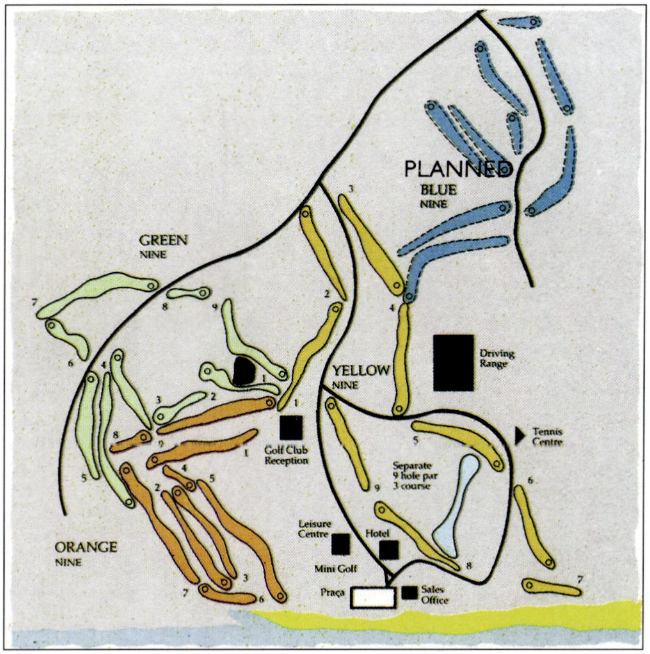

> *❛ Vale do Lobo's courses are amongst the best in Europe. The seventh hole on the Yellow Course is the most magnificent I have ever seen and it is the most photographed in the world. ❜*
>
> Judith Chalmers

YELLOW

Standard Scratch Scores
Yellow/Orange
Competition (White) Tees: 73
Regular (Yellow) Tees: 71
L.G.U. (Red) Tees: 73

	MEN						LADIES				
HOLE	COMP'N	REGULAR	PAR	STR	PLAYERS SCORE	MARKERS SCORE	DISTANCE	PAR	STR	PLAYERS SCORE	MARKERS SCORE
1	428	406	5	4			360	5	4		
2	292	280	4	8			270	4	6		
3	375	355	4	7			320	4	7		
4	366	344	4	1			309	4	1		
5	407	386	4	3			362	4	3		
6	296	288	4	9			268	4	8		
7	210	184	3	5			118	3	9		
8	378	357	4	2			321	5	2		
9	303	282	4	6			249	4	5		
	3055	2882	36				2577	37			
FIRST NINE											

ORANGE

Standard Scratch Scores
Orange/Green
Competition (White) Tees: 71
Regular (Yellow) Tees: 69
L.G.U. (Red) Tees: 70

	MEN						LADIES				
HOLE	COMP'N	REGULAR	PAR	STR	PLAYERS SCORE	MARKERS SCORE	DISTANCE	PAR	STR	PLAYERS SCORE	MARKERS SCORE
1	442	431	5	4			417	5	4		
2	397	351	4	1			345	4	1		
3	299	290	4	6			278	4	7		
4	155	144	3	9			124	3	9		
5	345	343	4	5			327	4	5		
6	178	174	3	7			135	3	8		
7	480	423	5	2			403	5	2		
8	137	133	3	8			123	3	6		
9	421	378	5	3			334	5	3		
	2854	2667	36				2486	36			
FIRST NINE											

GREEN

Standard Scratch Scores
Green/Yellow
Competition (White) Tees: 71
Regular (Yellow) Tees: 69
L.G.U. (Red) Tees: 70

	MEN						LADIES				
HOLE	COMP'N	REGULAR	PAR	STR	PLAYERS SCORE	MARKERS SCORE	DISTANCE	PAR	STR	PLAYERS SCORE	MARKERS SCORE
1	277	247	4	6			208	4	7		
2	187	173	3	7			131	3	6		
3	322	306	4	5			283	4	3		
4	473	466	5	1			412	5	1		
5	336	320	4	4			254	4	5		
6	141	139	3	8			106	3	8		
7	393	384	5	2			308	5	4		
8	135	129	3	9			112	3	9		
9	330	326	4	3			313	4	2		
	2594	2490	35				2127	35			
FIRST NINE											

Vila Sol

Pristine greens and delightful, distant distractions

Pages 58-9: View from behind 7th green

Vila Sol sprang to fame by hosting the 1992 Portuguese Open only eight months after its official opening - a magnificent achievement. Ronan Rafferty won the tournament with a breathtaking 40 foot birdie putt. Anders Forsbrand, who was the runner-up was only able to look on in amazement.

The greens are pristine and run true provided one takes sufficient care to read them properly. The course is one of the best kept in the Algarve. Although perhaps not the most imaginative course, it redeems itself with tight, testing holes requiring accurate long irons into the greens.

José Maria Cañizares had an inspired day during the 1992 Open -

Above: Approaching 14th green

Left: Looking north to distant hills, 7th hole left, 8th right

Far left: Main water holes, looking south

shooting an existing course record of 10 under par, 62. David Gilford won in 1993 after a play-off with Argentinian Jorge Berendt who had scored 63 in the first round.

Perhaps the most memorable hole is the par 5 sixth at 494 metres. The elevated tee looks down on a fairway scattered with bunkers and water hazards. It is easy to be distracted by spectacular views to the hills which form a distinct barrier between the Algarve and the Alentejo. No such distractions affected Martin Poxon when he achieved an amazing eagle during the 1993 Open. After taking a drop from the water hazard which intrudes into this fairway, he fired a long iron straight into the hole.

The following par 3 seventh is a very pretty but deceptive hole. Correct club

Opposite page: 2nd green

Left: Convenient leaning post

Below: Approaching 15th green

Right: Greens have to be read carefully

Below: Sol e Sombra

selection is paramount since the green is stepped and slopes severely from back to front. A long carry over water on this 180 metre hole tests accuracy and courage.

The par 5 eleventh demands controlled power and accuracy. At 456 metres it is not over long but undulations and a narrow fairway demand concentration.

Finally the par 4 seventeenth requires a blind drive to a narrow landing area bunkered left and treed rough on the right. The second shot to the green demands

Below: Careful course maintenance

great precision making this hole a really tough test. Any wayard shot is very severely punished and, coming so late in the round, stamina and determination win through.

The relatively comfortable eighteenth, although needing accuracy off the tee, lets you down gently. The inevitable post-mortem assures that you will want to experience the testing course at Vila Sol again - even if it's just to satisfy that nagging belief that you could do so much better next time.

COURSE INFORMATION

OWNED BY: *Empresa Imobiliária e Turística da Fonte Nova, S.A., Morgadinhos, Alto do Semino, 8125 Vilamoura. Tel: (089) 302144/5/6 Fax: (089) 302147*

GOLF DIRECTOR: *António Paixão*
PRO: *David Silva;*
ASSISTANT PRO: *Laurentino Mendes*

COURSE ARCHITECT: *Donald Steel*

FOUNDED: *1991*

NO. OF HOLES: *18*
Par (SSS): 72 (72)

LENGTH IN METRES: *6,189*

LAST IMPORTANT TOURNAMENT:
Portuguese Open 1992/3;
Lancôme Trophy 1993/94;
Johnnie Walker Euro Classic 1994.

GREEN FEES:
18 holes - 11,000$
9 holes - 6,000$

REQUIREMENTS TO PLAY AS A VISITOR: *Current handicap certificate. Max. men 27; ladies 35.*

AMENITIES

Pro shop
Driving range: 50 balls - 600$
Putting-greens (2)
Chipping green
Academy
Lessons: (members / non-members)
half hour - 4,000$ / 5,500$
one hour - 6,000$ / 8,000$
(including balls & clubs if required)
9 holes - 12,000$ / 14,000$
18 holes - 20,000$ / 22,000$
(including green fee)
Lockers
Club hire: 2,500$
Trolleys: 600$
Electric: 2,000$
Buggies: 18 holes - 7,000$
9 holes - 5,000$

CLUBHOUSE: *Attractively appointed building with spacious open terrace overlooking the eighteenth green. Contains all the usual amenities, pro shop, reception desk, trolley/ buggy storage, changing rooms, lounge, restaurant and bar. Recently extended to provide facilities for special functions.*

CATERING: *bar and restaurant.*
On course: bar and snacks beside ninth tee.

OTHER AMENITIES: *Tennis and Ancão Beach Club at Ria Formosa.*

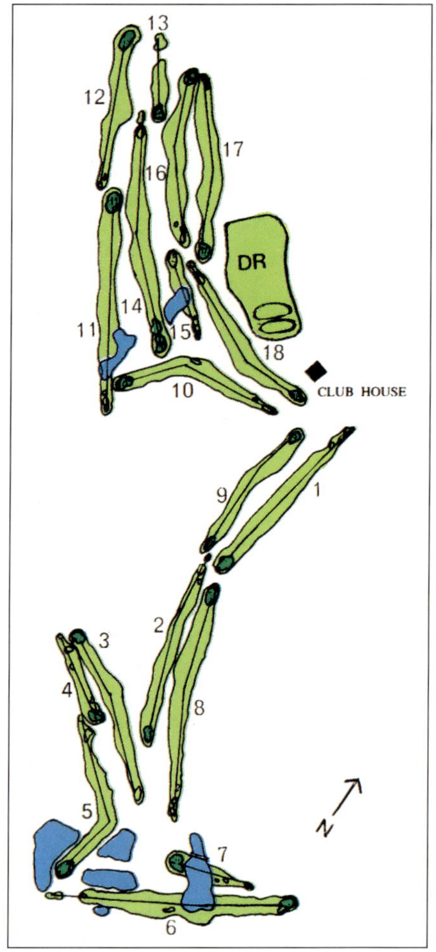

Vila Sol

S.S.S. 72

N.º	MTS.	MTS.	MTS.	PAR	STR.
1	381	366	344	4	5
2	407	367	345	4	3
3	385	372	349	4	1
4	190	158	117	3	9
5	362	331	321	4	15
6	494	480	418	5	7
7	180	162	125	3	11
8	499	483	411	5	13
9	292	284	274	4	17
OUT	3190	3003	2704	36	
10	355	342	307	4	8
11	456	446	409	5	16
12	313	301	284	4	18
13	159	150	144	3	14
14	458	432	422	5	4
15	177	161	135	3	10
16	346	338	328	4	12
17	369	349	291	4	2
18	366	358	314	4	6
IN	2999	2877	2634	36	
Total	6189	5880	5338	72	

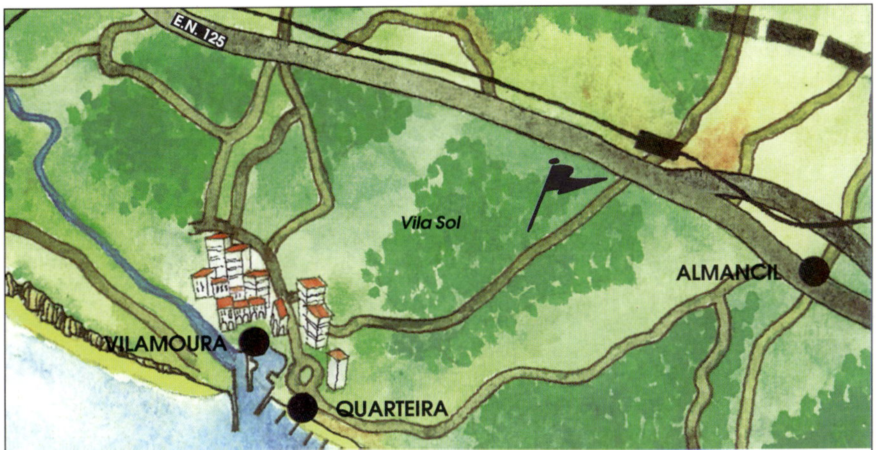

HOW TO FIND: *27 kms west of Faro airport. Turn south off the EN125 main road west of Almancil at "Quatro Estradas" (crossroads with traffic lights) towards Quarteira and Vilamoura. Vila Sol course is about a five minute drive from the crossroads, on right-hand side.*

OTHER ATTRACTIONS

Vilamoura - *Casino and plenty of good restaurants in the vicinity of Vilamoura marina; a variety of land as well as water sports facilities at Vilamoura.*
Quarteira - *Long beach and plenty of bars.*

"It's a nice course with a premium on accuracy."

Ronan Rafferty

"There are a lot of birdie chances, but you can get into some serious trouble with wayward tee shots."

Barry Lane, English professional

VILAMOURA I

Subtle changes and sweeping improvements to "old" course

Right: 18th hole with Clubhouse in background

Opposite page: 9th hole

Pages 68-9: 11th fairway

Vilamoura is Portugal's largest private leisure resort, with an area totalling some 4,000 acres. It houses, inter alia, three first class golf courses, a modern casino, a marina and an airstrip.

Vilamoura Um (One), also known as the "Old Course", is the longest established course in the resort. It was designed by the English golf architect Frank Pennink and opened in 1969. Over the years the fairways have subtly changed, becoming narrower and demanding a higher degree of accuracy. The reason quite simply is that the umbrella pines on or lining the fairways have grown extremely large over the years, both upwards and outwards.

No hole illustrates this quite as much as the par 4, 272-metre ninth where a precise drive is essential. Anything off-line either left or right ends up with a blocked approach to the severely sloping green in

Looking back down 8th fairway

view of the pinetrees and bunkers.

However, the delights of the par 3, fourth hole also illustrate Pennink's vision. At 154 metres it is not overly long, but what an approach! From the tee the shot must carry a lake, a huge pine tree and then a bunker protecting the green all across its entrance.

On the back nine, the eleventh at 392 metres is a challenging hole. A narrow landing area for the drive is produced by a bunker on the left and pine trees encroaching on both sides. The second demands a long iron shot to an elevated green protected once again by overhanging pines and a bunker on the right front. Accuracy is obviously required to ensure a good result, but it is an excellent testing par 4.

There are four par 5 holes on this loop and the 522-metre sixteenth is a fine test of length and straight hitting. The drive must be well positioned between tall pines to the right and a cross bunker on the left. The best line for the second shot is left of centre in order to open up an approach to the green.

The course hosted the Portuguese Open in 1970 and 1979, the Algarve Open

Below: 8th green

Opposite page: 11th on right, 8th and 9th on left

Left: 18th green

Below: Night play

in 1970, the World Ladies Amateur Championship in 1976 and the Portuguese Ladies Open in 1986.

Some extensive improvements are soon to be introduced, and the course will likely be closed for most of 1995. Golfers wishing to play on Vilamoura I are therefore advised to check beforehand whether it is open for play. A new automatic irrigation system, different strains of grass for tees, fairways and greens, and a refurbished or new clubhouse are the main changes planned, but the well known Vilamoura Old Course layout is fortunately being retained.

COURSE INFORMATION

OWNED BY: *Lusotur Golfes S.A., Vilamoura, 8125 Quarteira. Tel: (089) 321652, 389908 Fax: (089) 321262*

GOLF DIRECTOR: *Susete Calado*
PRO: *Joaquim Catarino*

COURSE ARCHITECT: *Frank Pennink*

FOUNDED: *1969*

NO. OF HOLES: *18*
Par (SSS): 73 (72)

LENGTH IN METRES: *6,331*

LAST IMPORTANT TOURNAMENT: *Johnnie Walker Euro Classic 1994*

GREEN FEES: *(Oct. 1994 to Sept. 1995) -*
Regular fee - 8,500$
Vilamoura Property owners and Juniors (up to 17-year-olds) - 4,500$
Members of Portuguese golf clubs - 5,000$
Multiple tickets (incl. complimentary 9-hole round) valid for all Vilamoura courses:
7 days, 5 rounds - 34,000$
10 days, 7 rounds - 42,000$
15 days, 10 rounds - 59,500$
*22 days, 15 rounds - 85,000$ **
*30 days, 20 rounds - 102,000$ **
** 25% extra discount for married couples when buying two multiple tickets.*

Reduced fee of 4,000$ - After 3 p.m. Dec. & Jan.; after 4 p.m. Feb., March, Oct. & Nov.; after 6 p.m. April to Sept.; and between 11 a.m. & 3 p.m. June to Sept.

REQUIREMENTS TO PLAY AS A VISITOR: *Handicap certificate. Dress code.*

AMENITIES

Pro shop

Driving range:	*50 balls**	*600$00*
	practice clubs	*500$00*

** One bucket free in five*
Putting-green

Lessons:	*half hour*	*3,500$00*
	one hour	*5,500$00*
Club hire:	*18 holes*	*3,500$00*
	9 holes	*2,000$00*
Trolleys: elect.	*18 holes*	*1,500$00*
	9 holes	*1,000$00*
hand	*18 holes*	*600$00*
	9 holes	*350$00*
Buggies	*18 holes*	*5,000$00*
	9 holes	*3,500$00*

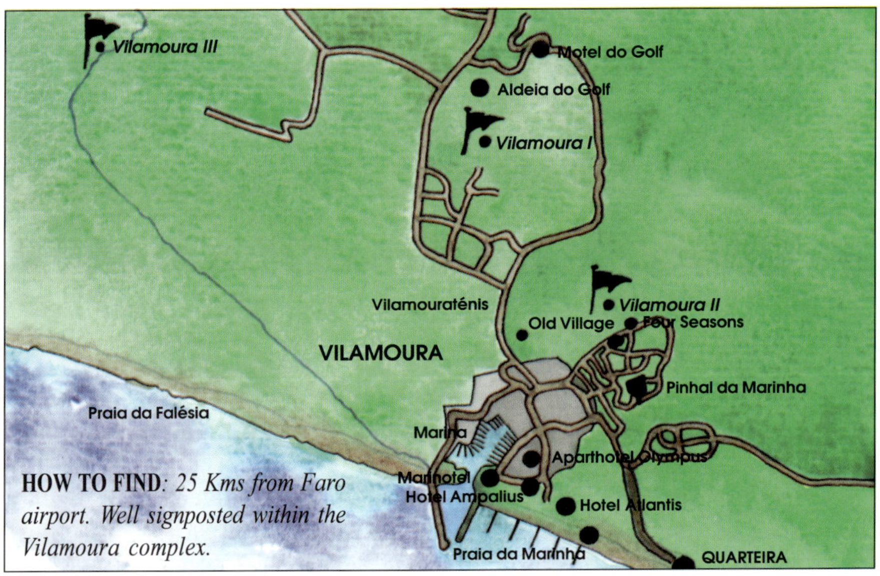

HOW TO FIND: *25 Kms from Faro airport. Well signposted within the Vilamoura complex.*

> *"Frank Pennink did a great job when he laid out this course. It is a very tough test indeed."*
>
> Bernard Hunt, former Algarve Open winner.

CLUBHOUSE: *Contains all usual amenities, pro shop, reception desk, starter's office. Open terrace area on ground level overlooking the eighteenth green, with bar serving drinks, snacks and indoor/outdoor restaurant for lunch.*

CATERING: *In clubhouse, as above. On course, by thirteenth tee.*

OTHER ATTRACTIONS

Vilamoura - *complex facilities include a marina, casino, hotels, many restaurants and bars; archaeological site (Roman); horse-riding, clay-pigeon shooting and tennis; water sports including game fishing; beaches.*

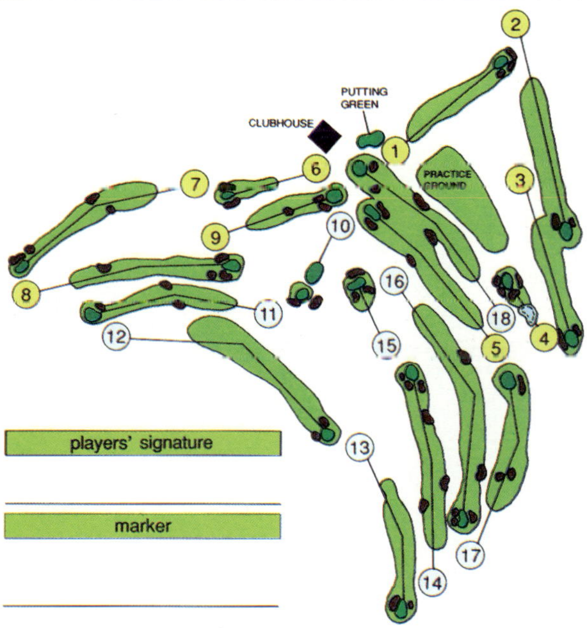

players' signature

marker

	marker	distance in meters			par	s.i.
1		271	266	254	4	17
2		452	442	350	5	5
3		333	322	258	4	9
4		154	144	109	3	15
5		416	336	320	4	3
6		214	207	164	3	11
7		396	354	333	4	7
8		429	404	362	4	1
9		272	262	249	4	13
Total		2937	2737	2399	35	out

	marker	distance in meters			par	s.i.
10		161	140	121	3	18
11		392	380	318	4	4
12		490	483	433	5	12
13		359	340	282	4	16
14		461	442	339	5	8
15		154	141	103	3	14
16		522	509	436	5	2
17		359	337	319	4	6
18		496	446	410	5	10
Total		3394	3218	2750	38	in

VILAMOURA II

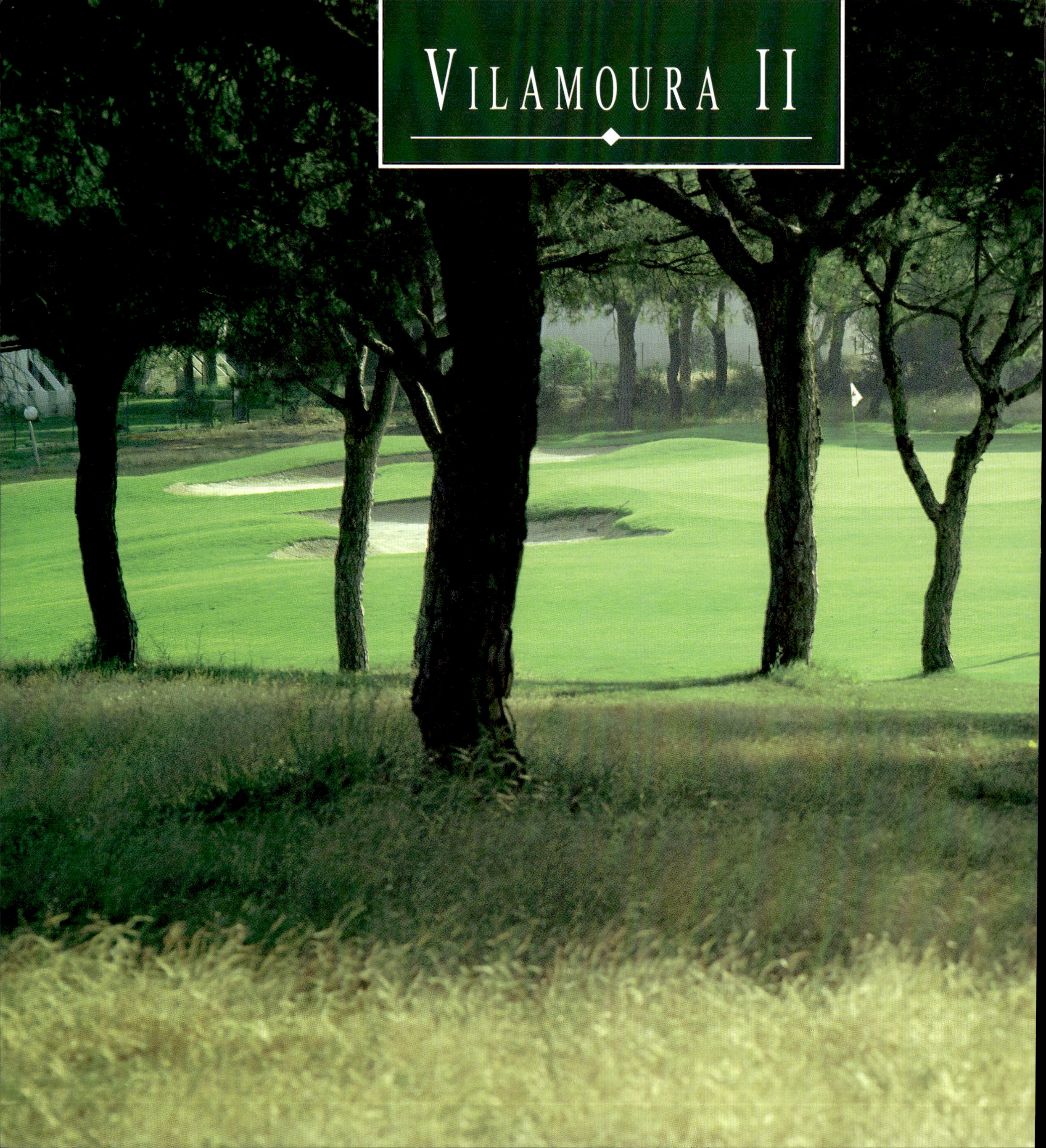

Pages 78-9: Approaching 4th green

Precision play among umbrella pines

This is another Pennink designed golf course, originally opened in 1976. Some reconstruction of several of the holes took place in 1985 under the direction of Robert Trent Jones, Jr. Although meandering through rolling countryside with umbrella pine lined fairways, it is more open than Vilamoura I. Smaller greens, however, maintain a requirement to play approach shots accurately.

The opening hole, a par 5 at 495 metres, has a generous fairway but a tricky, well protected, elevated and double-tiered green. To score well, a bold approach and correct club selection are paramount.

Right: 4th hole

Below: Tricky short 5th

The par 4 fourth at 348 metres again demands precision, and positioning off the tee is extremely important. Too long a drive and a lake to the right front of the green spells disaster. The second, a short iron approach shot over the corner of the lake to a severely contoured green is not for the faint-hearted. The green falls away on the left inviting a run off into greenside bunkers. To achieve par or better on this hole is a rewarding experience.

The longest hole on the course is the 518 metre par 5 thirteenth. It is stroke index 1, but not merely because of its length. From an elevated tee, the drive needs to be straight - deep rough on the left and pine trees on the right usually ensure a dropped shot for those who stray. The second is a blind shot over a rise in the fairway if you have the length. The approach area to the

Above: Daunting final green

Left: 5th green

Opposite page: Early morning light

Right: 10th green

Below: 9th green, practice area and clubhouse

putting surface is a vast flat plateau with greenside bunkers both left and front right. It is wise to check the distance marker here as the tendency is to underclub.

The 412 metre par 4 eighteenth is a fitting final hole. From a raised tee the ideal drive is over a rise in the fairway to ensure a view of the green at the foot of the slope. The second shot is the real test, a medium to long iron, to a green trapped at both sides of the entrance and at the back, with a step just forward of centre. This final approach shot at Vilamoura II is probably that most daunting of all, just when you thought you could relax!

COURSE INFORMATION

OWNED BY: *Lusotur Golfes S.A.*
Vilamoura,
8125 Quarteira.
Tel: (089) 321562
Fax: (089) 380726

GOLF DIRECTOR: *Susete Calado*
PRO: *Manuel Pardal*

COURSE ARCHITECT: *Frank Pennink*
Modifications by Robert Trent Jones, Jr.

FOUNDED: *1976*

NO. OF HOLES: *18. Par (SSS): 72 (71)*

LENGTH IN METRES: *6,256*

LAST IMPORTANT TOURNAMENT: *Johnnie Walker Euro Classic 1994*

GREEN FEES: *(Oct. 1994 to Sept. 1995)*
Regular fee - 8,500$
Vilamoura Property owners and Juniors (up to 17-year-olds) - 4,500$
Members of Portuguese golf clubs - 5,000$
Multiple tickets (including complimentary 9-hole round) for all three Vilamoura courses:
7 days, 5 rounds - 34,000$
10 days, 7 rounds - 42,500$
15 days, 10 rounds - 59,500$
*22 days, 15 rounds - 85,000$**
*30 days, 20 rounds - 102,000$**
** 25% extra discount for married couples when buying two multiple tickets.*
Reduced fee of 4,000$ - After 3 p.m. Dec. & Jan.; after 4 p.m. Feb., March, Oct. & Nov.; after 6 p.m. April to Sept.; and between 11 a.m. & 3 p.m. June to Sept.

REQUIREMENTS TO PLAY AS A VISITOR: *Handicap certificate. Dress code.*

AMENITIES

Pro shop			
Driving range:		*50 balls**	*600$00*
		practice clubs	*500$00*
** One bucket free in five*			
Putting-green			
Trolleys:	*elect.*	*18 holes*	*1,500$00*
		9 holes	*1,000$00*
	hand	*18 holes*	*600$00*
		9 holes	*350$00*
Buggies:		*18 holes*	*5,000$00*
		9 holes	*3,500$00*
Lessons:		*half hour*	*3,500$00*
		one hour	*5,500$00*
Club hire:		*18 holes*	*3,500$00*
		9 holes	*2,000$00*

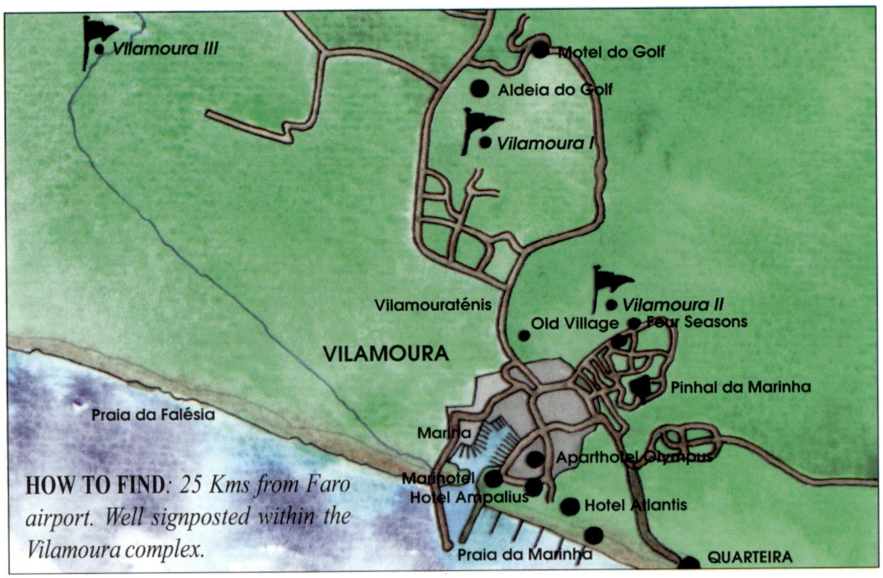

HOW TO FIND: *25 Kms from Faro airport. Well signposted within the Vilamoura complex.*

> *Vilamoura II is a beautiful course. Short game requires accurate play, greens are excellent and very tough. I am really impressed.*
>
> Peggy Conley, former Portuguese Ladies Open Champion

CLUBHOUSE: *Pro shop, reception, office, changing and locker rooms on ground floor. Pleasant terrace bar serving snacks, meals and drinks on upper level overlooking the driving range. Separate restaurant facility includes function room and lounge.*

CATERING: *Bar and restaurant at the clubhouse.*
On course: Bar/snacks located near seventh and thirteenth greens.

OTHER ATTRACTIONS

Vilamoura - *complex facilities include a marina, casino, hotels, many restaurants and bars; archaeological site (Roman); horse-riding, clay-pigeon shooting and tennis; water sports, including game fishing; beaches.*

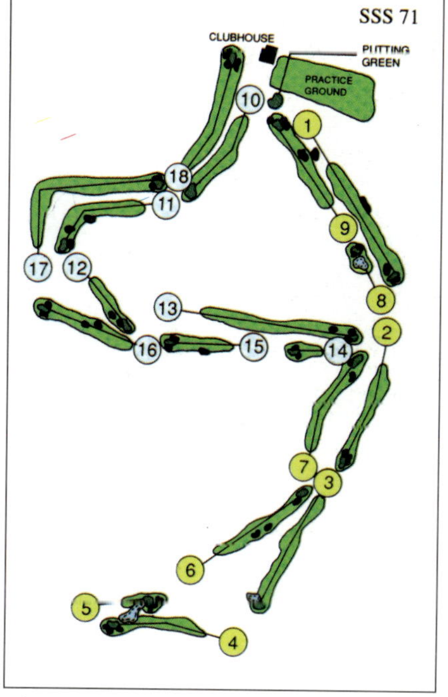

	marker	distance in meters			par	s.i.			
1		495	469	402	5	14			
2		398	374	339	4	4			
3		459	435	401	5	10			
4		348	318	279	4	8			
5		149	135	119	3	18			
6		394	382	324	4	2			
7		364	352	323	4	6			
8		149	131	108	3	12			
9		364	331	292	4	16			
Total		3120	2927	2587	36	out			

	marker	distance in meters			par	s.i.			
10		347	306	279	4	5			
11		336	324	274	4	11			
12		190	178	160	3	13			
13		518	508	494	5	1			
14		147	137	127	3	17			
15		341	330	275	4	15			
16		343	331	258	4	9			
17		502	492	472	5	3			
18		412	378	342	4	7			
Total		3136	2984	2681	36	in			

VILAMOURA III

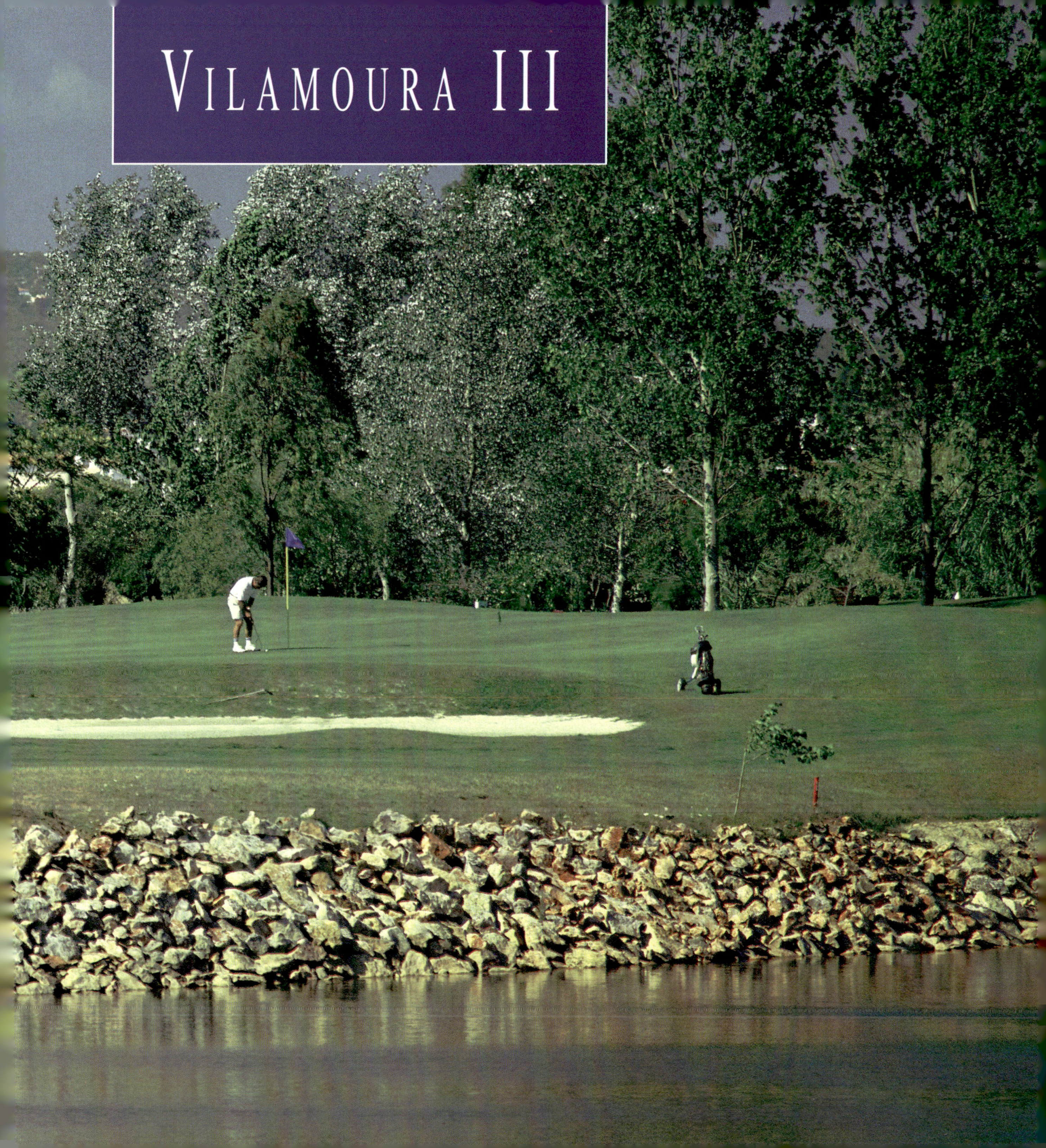

Triple treat, but watch the water

Above: Sunset on Marina course

Opposite page: 8th hole on Pinhal course

Pages 88-9: 4th hole on Lago course

Unlike the tree-lined courses of Vilamoura I and II, this is more reminiscent of a parkland course. Water hazards, however, play a major part in the layouts and often demand precise placing of both tee and fairway shots. Extensive fine tuning of greens, hazards and pathways have improved the overall appearance of all the three 9-hole courses of Vilamoura III.

The opening holes on Pinhal have broad fairways giving an impression of benign benevolence. Strategic bunkers however penalise the wayward and demand accurate approaches to the greens.

The sixth is a very tricky par 3 of a mere 118 metres. Depending on wind direction, however, club selection can be of vital importance. The tee and green are elevated, with the green being somewhat higher. A chasm of a bunker in front awaits the underclubbed or mis-hit shot. The green is further protected by a right-side bunker and one to the lower left back. A steeply

stepped section bisects the green making placement of the tee shot close to the pin difficult and putting perilous.

The teeth are well exposed on the final hole of Pinhal, a difficult par 4 of 399 metres. Water on the left and a long fairway bunker on the right ensure concentration off the tee. The second is a long iron or wood shot to the green. Water extends to the left front of the green and a steep bank invites the ball to run down into it. A narrow approach between this hazard and a greenside bunker on the right make this shot a test of accuracy and boldness.

The Lago course opens with a long par 5, well bunkered around and in front of the green, but the toughest hole must be the dog-legged fifth which is 315 metres long. The elevated tee faces out across an extensive lake, and a narrow strip of fairway on the left opens out into the landing area with the green off to the right. A confident drive crosses the water and lands short of several bunkers placed to catch any tee-shot that is too well struck. The tight approach to the green must cross fingers of the lake that extend into the fairway. Once again, club selection is very important: a most demanding hole and not one for the squeamish.

The par 5 eighth at 476 metres is a test of power and accurate approach. A blind tee shot over a rise should be aimed to the right side of the fairway to set up the second shot and achieve distance. The green is practically an island, surrounded not by water but bunkers protecting the lower front all round, and others catching the bold or

Page 92: Lago 9th hole

Page 93: Marina 9th and clubhouse

Opposite page: The biggest hazard on Marina is water

Below: Lago 5th green

over-clubbed shot at the back. The green always appears to be a tiny target from the fairway, and it's not that big once you are on it. What is normally required here is a high approach shot over the front bunkers, preferably with backspin.

The Marina course flows out towards the sand dunes protecting the flattish terrain from the sea. The lakes are full of bird-life and the reeds are a cacophony of natural sound. Wind is almost always present, gusting in off the sea or flowing down from the hills inland. This course has great variety, from pleasant undulating fairways to vicious dog-legs and water hazards. The latter are epitomised by the par 4 fifth hole, a 346 metre dog-leg with an extremely narrow landing area for the drive. With out-of-bounds on the left and a lake on the right, the pressure is on to place the tee-shot. The second stroke is across the lake to a green with a steep slope at the front and bunkered at the back. Depending on how you hit your drive, the second shot can either be a comfortable mid-iron or an awesome long iron.

The course doesn't let up easily, for the next hole is a 507 metre par 5 with water to the left and well in front. There is plenty of space for the drive and length is what is required. Bunkers on the right can catch the pushed or sliced drive. A channel of water bisects the fairway. The second shot is required to carry this and land on the fairway, now with a lake on the right. The approach needs to carry part of this lake and a dip in front of the green. Probably the most difficult hole of all the courses at Vilamoura III, but when played well gives so much satisfaction.

COURSE INFORMATION

OWNED BY: *Lusotur Golfes S.A.*
Vilamoura,
8125 Quarteira.
Tel: (089) 380722, 380724
Fax: (089) 380726

GOLF DIRECTOR: *Susete Calado*
PRO: *Abílio Coelho*

COURSE ARCHITECT: *Joseph Lee*

FOUNDED: *1990*

NO. OF HOLES: *27 (3 nine-hole loops: Pinhal, Lago and Marina).*
Par (SSS): 72 (71) each 18-hole combination

LENGTHS IN METRES: *Pinhal + Lago 5,888; Pinhal + Marina 6,115; Lago + Marina 6,133.*

LAST IMPORTANT TOURNAMENTS:
European Boys Team Championship 1994
Johnnie Walker Euro Classic 1994

GREEN FEES: *(Oct. 1994 to Sept. 1995)*
Regular fee - 6,500$
Vilamoura Property owners and Juniors (up to 17-year-olds) - 3,500$
Members of Portuguese clubs - 4,000$
Multiple tickets (incl. complimentary 9-hole round) valid for all three Vilamoura courses:

7 days, 5 rounds	*34,000$*
10 days, 7 rounds	*42,500$*
15 days, 10 rounds	*59,500$*
22 days, 15 rounds	*85,000$ **
30 days, 20 rounds	*102,000$ **

** 25% discount for married couples when buying two multiple tickets.*

Reduced fee of 3,000$ - After 3 p.m. Dec. & Jan.; after 4 p.m. Feb., March, Oct. & Nov.; after 6 p.m. April to Sept.; and between 11 a.m. & 3 p.m. June to Sept.

REQUIREMENTS TO PLAY AS A VISITOR: *Knowledge of golf etiquette.*

HOW TO FIND: *25 Kms from Faro airport. Well signposted within the Vilamoura complex, adjacent to the road to Albufeira.*

AMENITIES

Pro shop

Driving range:	*50 balls**	*600$00*
	practice clubs	*500$00*

** One bucket free in five*
Putting-green
Chipping -green
Academy

Lessons:	*half hour*	*3,500$00*
	one hour	*5,500$00*
Club hire:	*18 holes*	*3,500$00*
	9 holes	*2,000$00*
Trolleys: elect.	*18 holes*	*1,500$00*
	9 holes	*1,000$00*
hand	*18 holes*	*600$00*
	9 holes	*350$00*
Buggies	*18 holes*	*5,000$00*
	9 holes	*3,500$00*

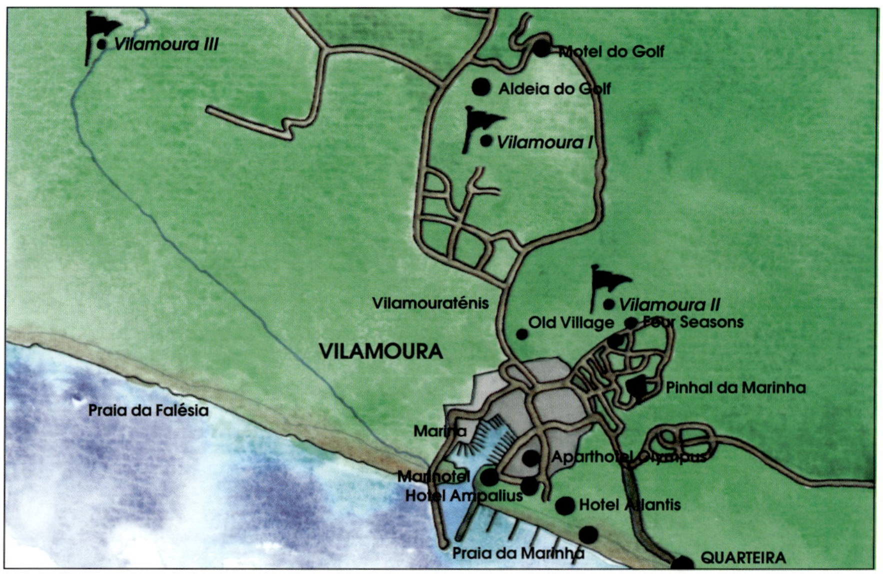

CLUBHOUSE: *Attractive, modern single storey building with terraces overlooking the ninth greens of Pinhal and Lago courses. Contains all usual amenities, pro shop, reception, changing and locker rooms, lounge, restaurant and bar. Function facilities available.*

CATERING: *Bar and restaurant in clubhouse. On course: Bar and snacks at eighth tee, Pinhal and sixth tee, Lago course.*

OTHER ATTRACTIONS

Vilamoura - *complex facilities include a marina, casino, hotels, many restaurants and bars; archaeological site (Roman); horse-riding, clay-pigeon shooting and tennis; water sports, including game fishing; beaches.*

> *"Vilamoura Três has a superb layout and some very challenging holes over the three nines. It will be among the best Portuguese courses in a few years time."*
>
> Henri Aeby, *Golf & Sport Events*

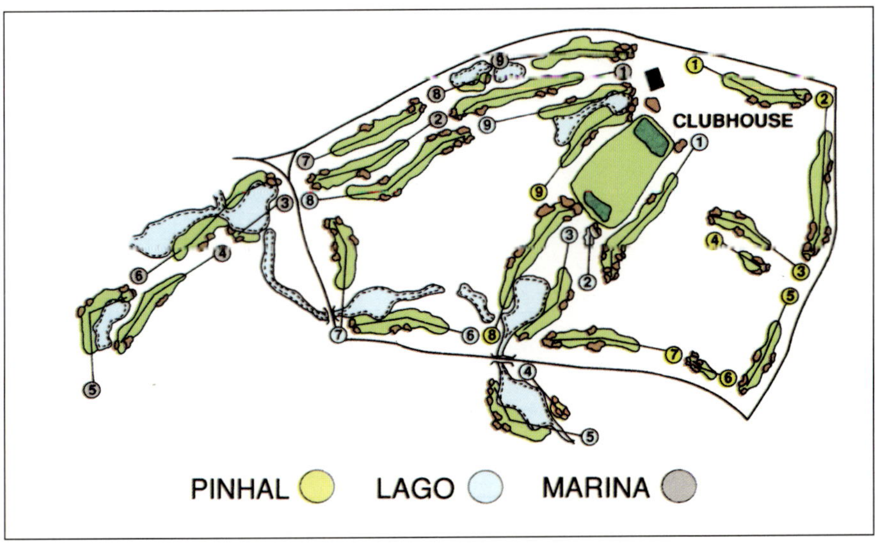

PINHAL

	marker	distance in meters			par	s.i.	scores		
1		348	328	281	4	6			
2		460	450	385	5	5			
3		309	290	247	4	9			
4		151	146	95	3	7			
5		321	316	266	4	4			
6		118	113	105	3	8			
7		376	360	304	4	2			
8		453	433	370	5	3			
9		399	380	325	4	1			
Total		2935	2816	2378	36				

LAGO

	marker	distance in meters			par	s.i.	scores		
1		472	453	402	5	8			
2		133	119	101	3	6			
3		357	342	322	4	2			
4		201	145	130	3	3			
5		315	298	220	4	4			
6		300	280	214	4	9			
7		321	303	235	4	5			
8		476	456	374	5	7			
9		378	364	325	4	1			
Total		2953	2760	2323	36				

MARINA

	marker	distance in meters			par	s.i.	scores		
1		484	460	415	5	9			
2		374	356	306	4	4			
3		178	145	118	3	3			
4		405	389	320	4	1			
5		346	328	284	4	2			
6		507	489	443	5	7			
7		354	334	284	4	8			
8		155	140	115	3	6			
9		377	360	295	4	5			
Total		3180	3001	2580	36				

PINE CLIFFS

Pages 98-9: 6th tee, 5th hole beyond

Below: Ocean view 5th

Clifftop caution, sheer pleasure

Left: 'Pulpit' 6th tee

Below: Overlooking Falésia beach

Pine Cliffs is an exclusive clifftop resort situated above Falésia, one of the Algarve loveliest beaches. The 5-star Sheraton Algarve Hotel overlooks the mass of umbrella pines lining the fairways of this delightful, holiday-style golf course. There is the added bonus of Atlantic Ocean views.

The location is convenient for visiting the tourist attractions of Albufeira, a bustling seaside town, and the resort of Vilamoura with its attractive marina. A lift gives easy access to the beach.

Back in 1990 Nigel Mansell liked to come here to escape the stress of the world's major motor racing circuits. He

Opposite page: 7th and Sheraton Hotel

came to Pine Cliffs to improve his golf in a relaxing atmosphere. He was elected President of what was then called Pine Cliffs Golf and Country Club. Playing off a two handicap he was frequently to be seen enjoying this delightful course with friends.

The times have moved on and so has Nigel, but the course here remains as challenging as ever. The first hole - a 328 metre par 4 - appears benign, but strategic bunker placement calls for accuracy and serves as an early lesson in concentration.

This is followed by a par 3, but the real testing starts with the third. A 310 metre dog-leg to the left with an incredibly narrow and defined landing area for the drive, bunkers, trees and a sloping fairway demand extremely precise placing. The second shot, uphill to a backward sloping green and guarded by bunkers in front, requires perfect club selection and positive striking of the ball.

The course generally is a good test of both concentration and ability, nowhere more so than on the spectacular par 3 sixth. From the back tee to green, a carry of some 205 metres, this demands a fearless stroke over a chasm hundreds of feet deep to a tricky undulating green.

Overall, the Pine Cliffs course is a challenging test and worthy of the time spent enjoying its vagaries.

Umbrella pines line fairways

COURSE INFORMATION

OWNED BY: *United Investments Portugal, Praia da Falésia, P.O.Box 644, 8200 Albufeira. Tel: (089) 501999 Fax: (089) 501950 Telex: 58524 PINECL P*

GOLF DIRECTOR: *David Marsh*
TEACHING PRO: *David Melville*

COURSE ARCHITECT: *Martin Hawtree*

FOUNDED: *1990*

NO. OF HOLES: *9.*
Par (SSS): [2 x 9] 66 (67)

LENGTH IN METRES: *2,324*

LAST IMPORTANT TOURNAMENT:
President's Trophy, 1992

GREEN FEES: *Hotel guests and property owners - 9 holes - 3,000$*
Visitors - 9 holes - 4,000$
Multiple advance green fees available at varying discounts.

REQUIREMENTS TO PLAY AS A VISITOR:
Current handicap certificate - 36 for both men and ladies.
Strict dress code, i.e. tailored shorts, collared shirts.

AMENITIES

Pro shop
Driving range: fee 600$ + balls 600$)
Putting-green
Chipping green
Academy

Lessons:	*30 minutes, one person*	*5,000$*
	50 minutes, one person	*9,000$*
	50 minutes, 2 persons	*10,000$*
	50 minutes, 3 persons	*11,000$*
Club hire:	*9 holes*	*1,750$*
	18 holes	*3,500$*
Trolleys:	*9 holes*	*600$*
	18 holes	*1,200$*
Buggies:	*9 holes*	*3,500$*
	18 holes	*7,000$*

CLUBHOUSE: *Small but adequate building opposite the first tee, with views from the open terrace towards the opening and closing holes and the putting-green. Reception desk in the pro shop; bar and restaurant serving drinks, snacks and buffet meals; changing rooms.*

CATERING: *bar and restaurant*

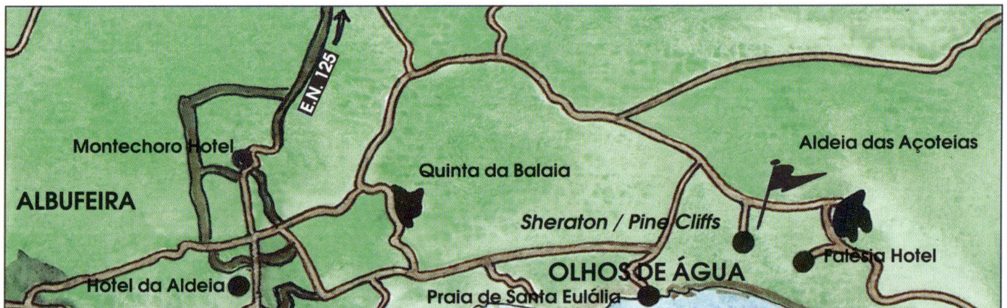

HOW TO FIND: *35 Km west of Faro airport signposted from EN 125 road to Sheraton Algarve, Praia da Falésia, near Aldeia das Açoteias. Halfway between Vilamoura and Albufeira.*

> ❛ This is not a course to play in a hurry. It's necessary to take time to savour the peace and magnitude of the place. ❜
>
> Martin Hawtree, course architect

OTHER ATTRACTIONS

A relaxed and particularly pleasing environment, yet not far from the tourist hubbub and central to all types of sports and leisure facilities geared to visitors.

Hole	White	Yellow	Par	S.I. Front 9	S.I. Back 9	Result		± Points	Result		Red	Par	S.I. Front 9	S.I. Back 9
1	328	279	4	13	14						256	4	13	14
2	148	139	3	11	12						111	3	11	12
3	310	294	4	3	4						281	4	3	4
4	138	121	3	17	18						86	3	17	18
5	400	343	5	1	2						254	4	1	2
6	205	149	3	5	6						128	3	5	6
7	360	321	4	7	8						298	4	7	8
8	280	256	4	9	10						236	4	9	10
9	155	149	3	15	16						134	3	15	16
	2324	**2051**	**33**								**1781**	**32**		
DISTANCE IN METRES			HANDICAP								ADD 10% FOR YARDS			
			RESULT											

S.S.S. MENS 67 LADIES 67

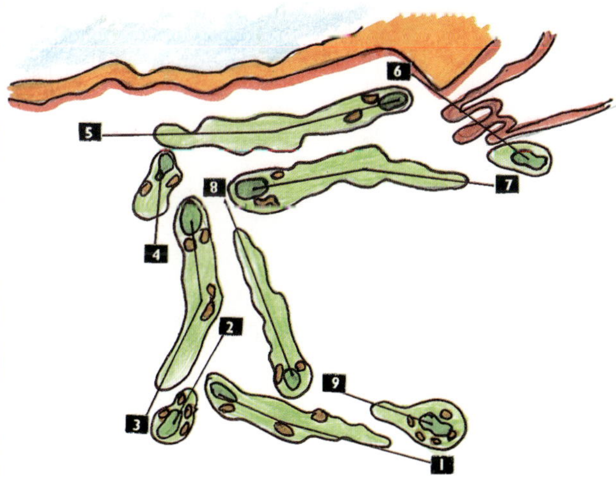

SALGADOS

Pages 106-7:
8th green

Right and below:
Lots of sun and water

Opposite page:
Early days. Course before maturity

Algarve's latest - links among lakes

Salgados is the newest golf course in the Algarve and the land on which it was built has a long and varied history. Converted from a former aircraft landing strip and wetland area adjacent to a bird sanctuary, much planning and design has resulted in a unique course.

It has the feel and ambience of a Scottish links course but with a Florida atmosphere - lots of sun and water. Lakes abound and most holes are influenced by water hazards. The course is compact and affords the golfer a true test of skill and accuracy.

Right: 3rd green

Below: 6th green

The third hole, a par 3, has water on both sides and a tight entrance to an unusual cross-shaped green. At only 170 metres from the championship tee, it appears uncomplicated, but undulations on the green make a par much more difficult to achieve.

The seventh, a testing par 4 of 415 metres, requires great precision from the tee and runs adjacent to the bird sanctuary. Wind and the narrowness of the fairway play an important role in the placing of the drive and subsequent second shot to the green. Rated as one of the best holes in Portugal, maturity can only improve its challenge.

The thirteenth, a dog-leg to the right, offers a choice to the confident golfer. Play safe from the tee to a wide landing area adjacent to water, or go for it over the water

Above:
Typical links terrain

Right:
Gentle undulations add interest

Chipping on to 4th green

straight to the green - 290 metres by the safe route or considerably less going for the hazardous one. The choice is yours!

The longest hole is the 545-metre par 5 fifteenth. The drive over a tidal creek, requires exact placing to avoid landing in dune hummocks lining the fairway. The second and third shots demand confidence and accuracy of approach.

The final three holes gently release the tension with wider fairways and benign hazards - an invitation to repeat an exciting experience.

Salgados has introduced an environmentally "green" concept to the Algarve for the first time. The irrigation water supply originates from waste generated from the town of Armação de Pera through a treatment plant built and installed at Salgados. This means that water is recycled and not drawn from precious supplies protected and conserved for other important uses.

COURSE INFORMATION

OWNED BY: *Hersal S.A.,*
Herdade dos Salgados,
Vale Rabelho,
Apartado 2266,
8200 Albufeira.
Tel: (089) 591111
Fax: (089) 591112

GOLF DIRECTOR AND PRO:
Peter Millhouse

COURSE ARCHITECT / DESIGNER:
Pedro de Vasconcellos and
Robert Muir-Graves

FOUNDED: *1994*

NO. OF HOLES: *18*
Par (SSS): 72 (72)

LENGTH IN METRES: *6,080*

GREEN FEES:
18 holes - 6,500$; 9 holes - 3,500$.
Members of Portuguese golf clubs -
18 holes - 5,000$; 9 holes - 3,000$.

REQUIREMENTS TO PLAY AS A VISITOR:
Knowledge of course etiquette.

AMENITIES

Pro shop
Driving range
Putting-green
Chipping green
Academy
Lessons

Trolleys:	*18 holes - 500$*
Club hire:	*full set, 18 holes - 3,000$*
	half set 18 holes - 2,000$
Buggies:	*9 holes - 3,000$*
	18 holes - 5,000$

■ *Special golf packages available from Almansor Hotel, Carvoeiro.*

CLUBHOUSE: *Modern purpose-built single storey building with light lunch facility served on terrace overlooking first tee, tenth tee, sixteenth green, seventeenth tee and eighteenth fairway. Bar serving lounge and terrace. Pro shop and reception entrance well appointed and carpeted. Changing rooms with locker facilities well laid out. Undercover buggy and trolley park.*

CATERING: *Bar and snacks catered by Almansor Hotel group. Beach bar.*

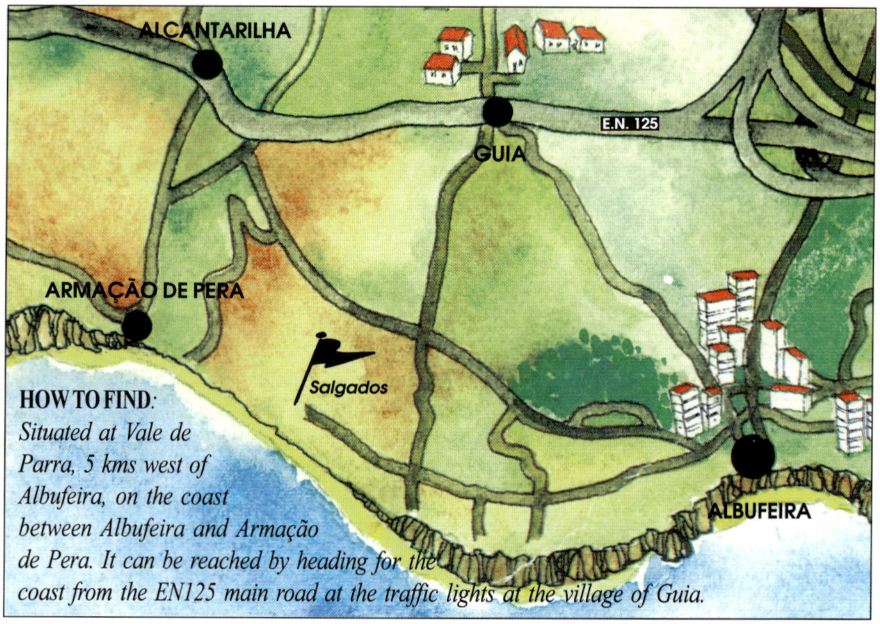

HOW TO FIND:
Situated at Vale de Parra, 5 kms west of Albufeira, on the coast between Albufeira and Armação de Pera. It can be reached by heading for the coast from the EN125 main road at the traffic lights at the village of Guia.

❛ Salgados is destined to become a favourite venue of rabbit, tiger, lounge lizard and naturalist. ❜

Peter Millhouse, course director.

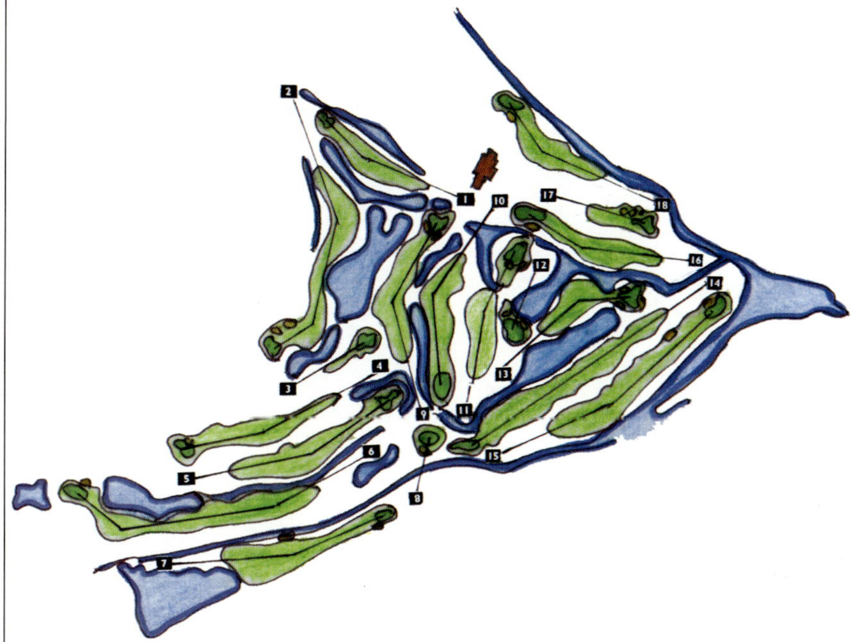

OTHER ATTRACTIONS

Albufeira - *the Algarve's busiest tourist town.*
Armação de Pera - *a resort town with plenty of bars and restaurants.*
Beaches - *one of the Algarve's longest stretches from Albufeira to Armação de Pera.*

HOLE	1	2	3	4	5	6	7	8	9	OUT
SSS72	320	485	170	360	375	515	415	135	350	3125
SSS69	280	455	150	350	350	480	390	120	325	2900
SSS72	260	430	130	320	320	445	345	105	300	2655
SSS69	240	405	110	285	300	430	305	90	285	2450
PAR	4	5	3	4	4	5	4	3	4	36
STROKE	11	5	15	9	7	3	1	17	13	

HOLE	10	11	12	13	14	15	16	17	18	IN	TOT	HCP NET
SSS72	390	300	130	295	490	545	320	180	305	2995	6080	
SSS69	360	285	115	265	455	515	305	160	280	2740	5640	
SSS72	340	260	107	255	430	435	285	140	250	2502	5157	
SSS69	300	235	96	225	410	405	240	125	225	2261	4711	
PAR	4	4	3	4	5	5	4	3	4	36	72	
STROKE	6	10	18	8	4	2	14	16	12			

Vale de Milho

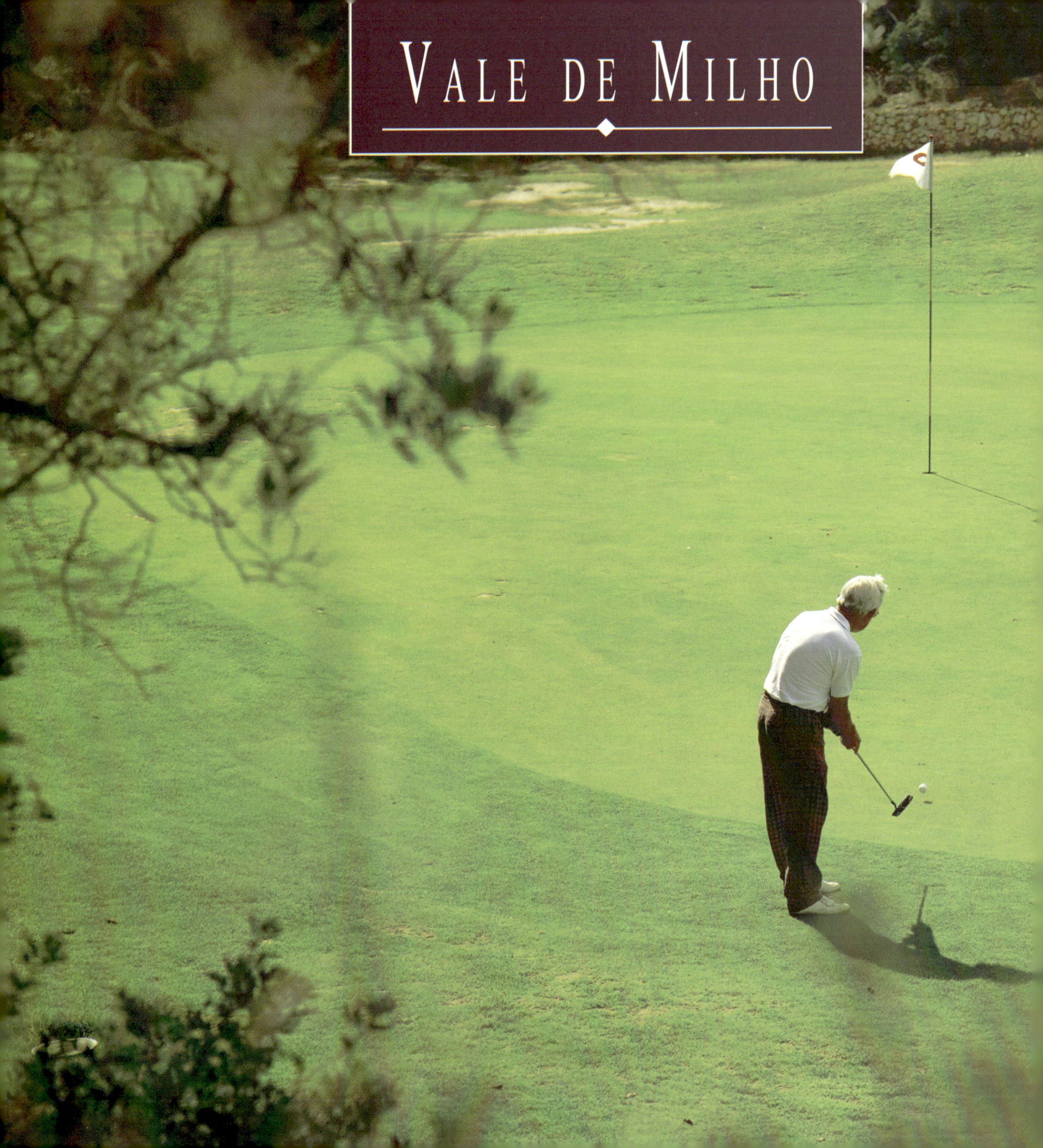

Opposite page: 2nd green

Left: 1st green

Short shots to sharpen your swing

This is an ideal little par 3 course suitable for beginners, holiday-makers or golfers interested in sharpening their short game.

Hole lengths range from a mere 60 metres to the longest one at 164 metres, and the greens and bunkers are a reasonable size, comparable to some on full-size courses.

Below: Cascading water hazard

Also on the course are attractive water hazards which add a touch of difficulty, or at least make the golfer pay attention.

This applies especially to the second hole where water cascades down from the left in a stone wall-lined stream into the large lake on the right. With trees on the left, the entrance to the green is tight as a bunker also guards the right front side. An interesting feature in the clubhouse is the sophisticated golf swing laboratory with computer analysis, etc. Golfers can take away videos of their swing action, with the pro's advice recorded on them.

Right: Playing 2nd hole

Below: View from behind 1st green with 3rd fairway in background

COURSE INFORMATION

OWNED BY: *Multiger, S.A., Sociedade de Compra, Venda e Administração de Propriedades, S.A., Apartado 273, Praia do Carvoeiro, 8400 Lagoa. Tel: (082) 358502 Fax: (082)358497*

MANAGED BY: *Gericonstroi, S.A., Administração, Construção, Compra e Venda de Imóveis, S.A.*

GOLF DIRECTOR / SECRETARY: *Mrs. Christine Kenyon*
PRO'S: *Norman Wharton, and Carlos Ribeiro*

COURSE ARCHITECT: *David Thomas*

FOUNDED: *1990*

NO. OF HOLES: *9 (two sets of tees)*
Par (SSS) - 2 x 9: 54 (54)

LENGTH IN METRES: *926 (919 2nd time round)*

GREEN FEES: *(For 1994/5 season)*
9 holes - 2,250$ 18 holes - 3,250$
Under 18-years-old
9 holes - 1,750$ 18 holes - 2,500$.
7-round season tickets available at a discount, e.g. 7 x 18 holes 17,500$

REQUIREMENTS TO PLAY AS A VISITOR: *Knowledge of golf and etiquette rules.*

AMENITIES

Pro shop
Driving range
Putting-green
Chipping green w/practice bunker
Academy with golf swing laboratories
Lessons
Club hire: 18 holes - 2,500$
Trolleys: 18 holes - 350$
Locker room facilities

CLUBHOUSE: *Spacious, with large verandah overlooking four holes. Large bar and restaurant area, changing rooms, pro shop, games area (snooker, darts, etc).*

CATERING: *At bar and restaurant in club-house. Both lunch and dinner served.*

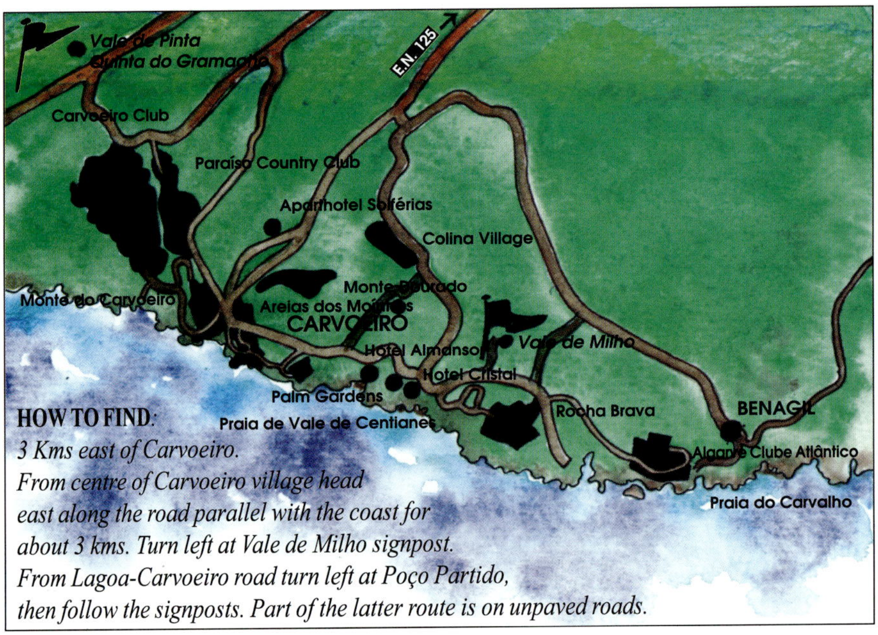

HOW TO FIND: *3 Kms east of Carvoeiro. From centre of Carvoeiro village head east along the road parallel with the coast for about 3 kms. Turn left at Vale de Milho signpost. From Lagoa-Carvoeiro road turn left at Poço Partido, then follow the signposts. Part of the latter route is on unpaved roads.*

OTHER ATTRACTIONS

Carvoeiro - *is a bustling tourist village during the summer, quiet in winter, with a good choice of restaurants.*

Beaches - *several excellent beaches nearby, the nearest to the golf course being at Vale de Centianes.*

❛ *I thought we should produce a 9-hole course which players can get around using only irons. A landscaped garden effect, with various water features to play around, provides a challenge to all players.* ❜

David Thomas, course architect

Vale de Milho

BURACO HOLE	RESULTADO MARCADOR MARKERS SCORE	MET YELLOW	PAR	STR.	RESULTADO SCORE		
1		110	3	5			
2		154	3	2			
3		68	3	17			
4		86	3	12			
5		116	3	7			
6		75	3	16			
7		95	3	10			
8		88	3	14			
9		134	3	3			
	SAÍDA/*OUT*	926	27				

ASSINATURA DE MARCADOR:
MARKERS SIGNATURE: ____________

ASSINATURA DO JOGADOR:
PLAYERS SIGNATURE: ____________

BURACO HOLE	RESULTADO MARCADOR MARKERS SCORE	MET RED	PAR	STR.	RESULTADO SCORE		
10		90	3	6			
11		164	3	1			
12		60	3	18			
13		97	3	11			
14		106	3	8			
15		94	3	15			
16		102	3	9			
17		96	3	13			
18		110	3	4			
	VOLTA/*IN*	919	27				
	SAÍDA/*OUT*	926	27				
	TOTAL	1845	54				
	HANDICAP						
	NET						

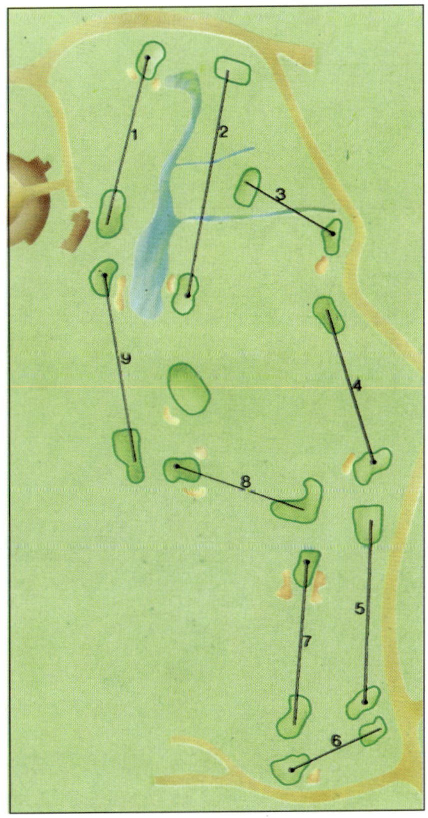

Quinta do Gramacho

Double nine design, a first in Europe

The only common components between the first and second rounds on this course are the fairways - there are only nine of them, but golfers play off different sets of tees to different greens on each nine.

Confusing? A little, perhaps, but the variety of tee and green placings on this 'double-nine' course make most of the holes appear completely dissimilar. As Gramacho is the only course of this type in Europe, it is well worthwhile trying it out for a round or two.

Above: Breezy day on 5th and 14th

Opposite page: 1st and 10th green

Pages 122-3: 14th green

Opposite page: 3rd & 12th green with clubhouse and Monchique hills in background

Right: Temporary clubhouse by closing greens

Like its sister course, the conventional 18-hole Vale de Pinta on the same site, there are four sets of tees for each of the eighteen individual holes. Players can choose the tees which best suit their ability.

Although ideal for holiday golf, Gramacho includes some fine testing holes, for example the par five second (eleventh second time round) measuring 490 metres. Played from the eleventh tee to the corresponding green - this one is actually a double, St. Andrews style - the length is 506 metres. Two large fairway pine trees attract the drive, and a mass of largish bunkers before the vast, contoured green force most golfers to lay up on the second shot.

Like the short par four opening hole, the fifth has an outcrop of rocks with trees and scrub right in the middle of the split fairway. You aim left first time round and right on the second round.

The seventh is stroke index 1 and demands two straight shots, the approach normally requiring a mid- to long-iron to a green well defended by bunkers. An ancient well on the right of the fairway has been left as a decorative feature.

Before the uphill ninth (or eighteenth) par 5, there is a short par 4 with a narrow fairway where it is advisable for long hitters to take a mid-iron from the tee. On the first round, the approach is played boldly over a large lake on the left to a terraced green.

AMENITIES

Pro shop
Driving range: *50 balls - 500$*
Putting-green
Chipping green
Academy
Lessons: *half hour - 3,500$; 50 mins - 6,000$*
Club hire: *2,500$*
Trolleys: *9 holes - 500$; 18 holes - 750$*
Electric trolleys: *9 holes - 1,500$; 18 holes - 2,500$*

CLUBHOUSE: *Temporary clubhouse with cosy atmosphere, overlooking the ninth and eighteenth greens. Reception desk for both this and Vale de Pinta courses, real estate sales office, changing rooms, pro shop, and bar/restaurant with outside terrace.*

CATERING: *Drinks, snacks and light meals at clubhouse.*

OTHER ATTRACTIONS

Beaches *and* **fishing villages** - *Several nearby along the coast under splendid cliffs.*
Carvoeiro - *nearby tourist village with a wide selection of restaurants.*
Lagoa - *a pleasant market town and centre of wine production.*

COURSE INFORMATION

OWNED BY: *Carvoeiro Golfe, S.A., Apartado 24, 8400 Lagoa. Tel. (082) 342168 Fax. (082) 342189*

GOLF DIRECTOR: *Stuart Woodman*
SECRETARY: *Isabel Ferreira*
PRO'S: *Roel Gritter and Paul Tipper*

COURSE ARCHITECT: *Ronald Fream*

FOUNDED: *December, 1991*

NO. OF HOLES: *18 (Double nine)*
Par (SSS): 72 (71)

LENGTH IN METRES: *5,919*

GREEN FEES: *(Valid until May 1995)*
9 holes - 5,000$; 18 holes- 8,000$.
Multiple green fees available at a discount.

REQUIREMENTS TO PLAY AS A VISITOR:
Max. handicap 36 for both men and ladies.

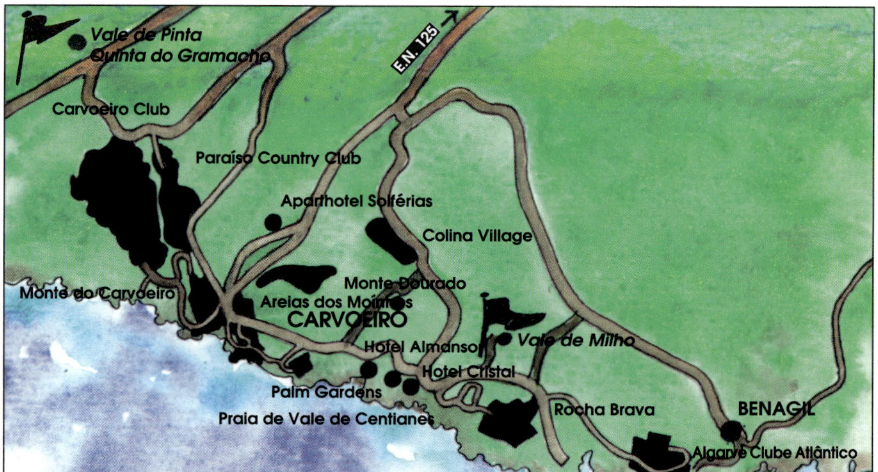

HOW TO FIND: *Turn off the EN125 main road from Lagoa to Carvoeiro. Take the right fork after 300 metres and follow the signs to Carvoeiro Golfe. Clubhouse is about 5 kms from the fork.*

HOLE	DISTANCE IN METRES				PAR	S.I.
1	310	289	268	244	4	12
2	490	462	440	410	5	4
3	339	309	307	284	4	14
4	186	162	130	115	3	18
5	327	305	285	262	4	6
6	178	169	150	132	3	15
7	376	353	341	325	4	1
8	284	268	246	217	4	8
9	482	452	424	395	5	10
OUT	2972	2769	2591	2384	36	
HOLE	DISTANCE IN METRES				PAR	S.I.
10	338	317	302	275	4	11
11	506	476	456	426	5	3
12	299	273	268	244	4	13
13	186	150	115	99	3	17
14	347	321	305	282	4	5
15	159	147	126	110	3	16
16	363	346	333	312	4	2
17	291	278	258	228	4	7
18	458	428	400	373	5	9
IN	2947	2736	2563	2349	36	

Quinta do Gramacho

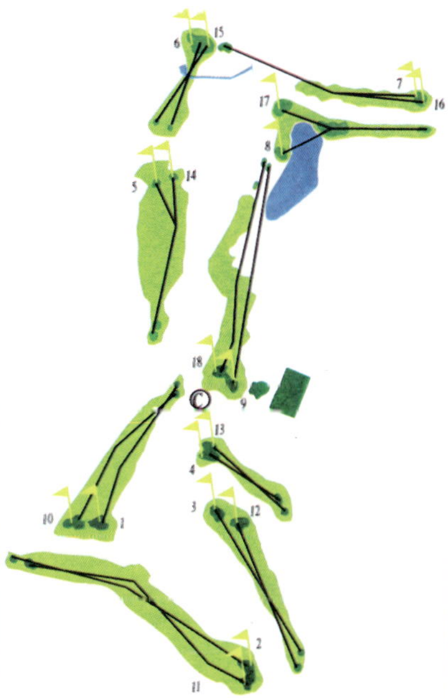

I live close to Augusta National Golf Course and play there quite regularly. I'll warn our superintendent! Your greens at Gramacho are as good as Augusta!

Jack Warner, visiting golfer.

I have read the comments of Mr. Warner re Augusta and he's right. There are not many courses the European Tour visit that can match the quality of Gramacho's greens.

Andy McFee, Senior Tour Director,
PGA European Tour.

Vale de Pinta

Pages 130-1: 13th green

Opposite page: Par 3 2nd

Right: Your target on hole one

Below: Ancient olive

Fream's dream amid ancient olive groves

As soon as he saw it, Californian golf architect Ronald Fream fell in love with this rural site which was to be transformed into one of his most masterful course designs. Full advantage was taken of the natural valleys and undulations of the terrain. Nearly all the centuries-old olive trees were retained - sometimes in the middle of the hybrid bermuda grass fairways - and many were successfully transplanted. Fig, almond and carob trees also abound on this very attractive course which has matured well in the short period it has been open for play.

At present, Vale de Pinta is served by the temporary clubhouse at the adjacent

Quinta do Gramacho course. When the Vale de Pinta clubhouse is built on a site between the current thirteenth and fourteenth holes, the latter will become the opening hole and the fifteenth the future second, etc.

An interesting feature is the variety of tees available - yellow, white and black markers for the men, in addition to the ladies' red ones. The total length from the yellow markers is only 4,958 metres. From the white ones it is 5,382 metres which is 479 less than that measured from the black 'tiger' tees.

The par 3 second measuring 184 metres from the black tee is a pretty hole played over a valley to a large, wide and contoured green. Avoid being trapped in the deep bunkers before the green. A friendly bank at the back will normally guide an over-hit ball back on to the putting surface.

One needs a long drive from the elevated fourth tee to clear the olive trees down in a dip to set up a birdie chance on this scenic 361-metre dog-leg hole. There is an escape route to a restricted landing area on the right.

The eighth is a short par 4 fraught with danger from tee to green. To drive directly to the green you play over a large lake but on the far bank there are large rocks, an enormous bunker as well as trees. Bunkers also protect the right-hand side of the fairway and the left of the tricky, fast green. A birdie or even par here is normally well earned.

Left: Olive trees bathed in evening sunlight

11th green

Opposite page: 11th and 12th holes

Another unusual short par 4 is the uphill 323-metre eleventh which demands a well placed tee shot. With bunkers and trees in the centre of the fairway you can go for broke up the narrow right-hand side to set up a birdie chance, but a clump of bushes on the right can lead to trouble. The long, narrow sloping green is deceptive for both approaching and putting.

Although the thirteenth is the longest hole at 541 metres, it is fairly flat through a valley of ancient gnarled olive trees. It is claimed that one not far from the green on the left is about 1,500 years old, dating from the very start of the middle ages.

The sixteenth is a beautiful dog-leg left which is laid out before you from the raised tee, giving a picture of the task in hand. If you are tempted to cut the corner, trees and a myriad of bunkers are a serious threat. Although there is not too much room on the right, the safe drive will leave a mid iron to the treacherous split level green.

The course closes with a good par 5 with a narrow fairway, and then a nerve-tingling par 3 only 126 metres long and played down towards a green with a menacing lake immediately behind it.

Left: Massive bunker guards 10th green

HOLE	DISTANCE IN METRES				PAR	S.I.
1	359	337	316	293	4	8
2	184	166	142	116	3	16
3	330	307	293	281	4	14
4	361	325	289	261	4	4
5	362	332	301	277	4	2
6	148	140	127	120	3	18
7	455	415	387	363	5	6
8	310	278	262	253	4	10
9	468	445	397	340	5	12
OUT	2977	2745	2514	2304	36	
10	179	139	136	116	3	15
11	323	302	277	259	4	5
12	170	147	128	111	3	13
13	541	512	475	441	5	1
14	319	287	267	239	4	11
15	353	324	302	280	4	9
16	351	332	311	277	4	7
17	522	487	453	414	5	3
18	126	107	95	87	3	17
IN	2884	2637	2444	2224	35	
OUT	2977	2745	2514	2304	36	
TOTAL	5861	5382	4958	4528	71	

COURSE INFORMATION

OWNED BY: *Carvoeiro Golfe, S.A., Apartado 24, P-8400 Lagoa, Tel: (082) 342168 Fax: (082) 342189*

GOLF DIRECTOR: *Stuart Woodman*
SECRETARY: *Isabel Ferreira*
PRO'S: *Roel Gritter and Paul Tipper*

COURSE ARCHITECT: *Ronald Fream*

FOUNDED: *1992*

NO. OF HOLES: *18. Par (SSS): 71 (71)*

LENGTH IN METRES: *5,861*

LAST IMPORTANT TOURNAMENT: *1993 TAP (Air Portugal) Amateur Open*

GREEN FEES: *(Valid until May 1995) 8,000$. Multiple green fees available at a discount.*

REQUIREMENTS TO PLAY AS A VISITOR: *Max. handicap - men 28, ladies 34.*

AMENITIES

Pro shop
Driving range: 50 balls - 500$
Putting-green
Chipping green
Academy
Lessons: half hour - 3,500$; 50 mins - 6,000$
Club hire: 2,500$
Trolleys: 750$
Electric trolleys: 2,500$
Buggies: 5,500$

CLUBHOUSE: *Temporary clubhouse overlooking ninth/eighteenth greens at Quinta do Gramacho course (400 metres from first tee of Vale de Pinta course). Small, cosy clubhouse with reception desk for both courses, real estate sales office, changing rooms, pro shop, bar/restaurant with outdoor terrace.*

CATERING: *Drinks, snacks and light meals at clubhouse. Beverage machine near seventh green.*

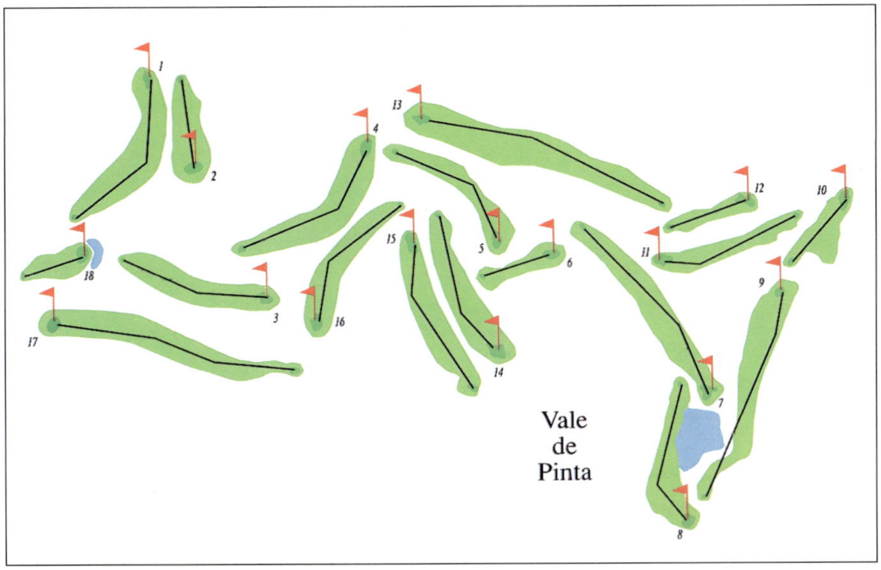

> *Vale de Pinta is on God-given land. It is one of the finest courses I have ever done.*
>
> Ronald Fream,
> course architect.

OTHER ATTRACTIONS

Fishing villages *and* **beaches** - *several dotted along the coast under splendid cliffs.*
Carvoeiro - *nearby tourist village (pictured below) has a wide selection of restaurants.*
Lagoa - *a pleasant market town, a centre of wine production.*

HOW TO FIND: *Turn off the EN125 main road from Lagoa to Carvoeiro. Take the right fork after 300 metres and follow the signs to Carvoeiro Golfe. Clubhouse is about 5 kms from the fork.*

Alto Golf

'Serpent' and 'giant' in peaceful parkland

Right: Across the 'Giant' 16 th, to 10th green

Opposite pages: 2nd fairway with bread oven

The Alto Golf course is located in an attractive area steeped in golfing tradition. Just a few kilometres away is the area where the game was first played in the Algarve, a long extinct, rudimentary layout with sand and oil greens, or "browns", dating back to the 1920's between Portimão and Praia da Rocha. Alto is also less than seven kilometres from the venerable Penina, Algarve's first grass golf course.

Like Penina, Alto was designed by Sir Henry Cotton, British Open champion in 1934, 1937 and 1948, who made the Algarve his home back in the sixties. This was his last 18-hole course design, and construction started shortly before the old maestro passed away in December, 1987.

Page 140-1: the 'Serpent'

The course was opened in 1991 by Portugal's President Mário Soares who made the inaugural stroke with a driver which is on display in the clubhouse.

Built on ideal, undulating terrain amongst traditional vineyards close to the coast, Alto is blessed with fine views of both the sea and the Monchique range of hills in the hinterland. Nearby is the fishing village of Alvor at the estuary of a river of the same name.

Many golfers may disagree with a course design featuring a par 3 opening hole, but this immediately puts a premium on accuracy, a typical Cotton trait encountered on this course. It is advisable, therefore,

for golfers to be properly warmed up before venturing to the first tee.

Hidden bunkers threaten on the left of the first hole and a steep drop beyond the green is an added danger if one overclubs.

The fourth and fifth are interesting holes. The fourth is a par 4 played across a valley with a lake to the right, which is the recommended side of the fairway to take. By doing so you avoid being blocked out by a copse on the left for the challenging approach shot, which is uphill to a tricky, sloping green.

As with many courses elsewhere in Europe, the Alto holes feature interesting names. The double dog-leg par 5 fifth was aptly dubbed in Portuguese '*A Serpente*'. On the right, the sixth hole is out-of-bounds. This precludes taking an alternative route. On the left, two bunkers at the edge of the

7th tee off

Opposite page: 3rd hole

Bird's-eye view of first nine

rough await errant tee-shots. The left-hand side also incorporates a stretch of out-of-bounds territory almost up to the large green, protected only by a single bunker well short of the putting surface on the left of the fairway.

The back nine start with a challenging par 4 which measures 410 metres from the championship tee. It demands a precise drive, flirting with the out-of-bounds area to the right, to land on the fairway without running downhill to the trees on the left. If you shoot too far right you will be stymied by tall pine trees. In approaching the elevated green from the sloping fairway, another accurate shot is required if you are to score well on this memorable hole.

The par 4 fifteenth with a blind shot off the tee and an up-hill approach to a split-level green is a good test of golf, but just wait for the following hole which justifies being called the 'Giant'. At 604 metres (660 yards) from the championship tee, it is reputed to be the longest hole in Europe. Those who dare attempt the long drive are

faced with a bottle-neck in the fairway between the out-of-bounds markers on the right and a lake on the left, not forgetting the olive trees dotted around. Once these hazards have been negotiated there is still a long straight stretch of fairway until you finally reach the green, which is well defended by three bunkers and a steep slope down to the left.

The 'Giant' is also known as the "Henry Cotton Challenge". Before going out on to the course, golfers can apply at the clubhouse reception desk to make an official attempt to score a birdie. Those who succeed secure a certificate to that effect, as well as having their name engraved on a special board in the clubhouse.

An unusual detail on the course is an old bread oven located on the left-hand side of the second fairway. It is not so much an ethnological attraction as an immovable obstruction. Another decorative touch is the design of the hole distance markers on the tees. They are made from colourful tiles integrated into white bases.

A total of about 10,000 trees and shrubs were planted on the course, creating parkland surroundings which, together with the man-made lakes, have attracted many species of birds to the area.

10th fairway

COURSE INFORMATION

OWNED BY: *HOTAL, S.A.,*
Quinta do Alto do Poço,
Apartado 1, Alvor,
8500 Portimão.
Tel: (082) 416913, 401045
Fax: (082) 401046

GOLF DIRECTOR: *Christopher Stilwell*
PRO: *Robert Bridge*

COURSE ARCHITECT: *Sir Henry Cotton*

FOUNDED: *1991*

NO. OF HOLES:
18. Par and SSS: 72 (73)

LENGTH IN METRES: *6,125 metres.*

LAST IMPORTANT TOURNAMENT: *TAP (Air Portugal) Amateur Open 1993*

GREEN FEES: *(valid until October 1 1995)*
9 holes - 4,600$; 18 holes - 7,950$.
Juniors under the age of 18 are entitled to a 50% reduction.

REQUIREMENTS TO PLAY AS A VISITOR: *Current handicap certificate.*

HOW TO FIND: *Situated about midway between Alvor and Portimão. Keep an eye out for large Alto Golf display boards and directional signposts.*

AMENITIES

Pro shop — *Academy*
Driving range: 50 balls - 600$
Putting-green
Chipping green — *Trolleys: 600$*
Lessons: half hour - 4,000$
Practice clubs: each club per session - 350$
Buggies: 9 holes - 3,200$; 18 holes - 5,000$

CLUBHOUSE: *Comprises reception desk, office, pro shop, indoor bar, outdoor terrace, changing rooms, as well as real estate sales and display area. The clubhouse is set amongst attractive gardens overlooking the eighteenth green. Practically the entire back nine holes can be viewed from the terrace.*

CATERING: *Bar and snacks in the clubhouse*

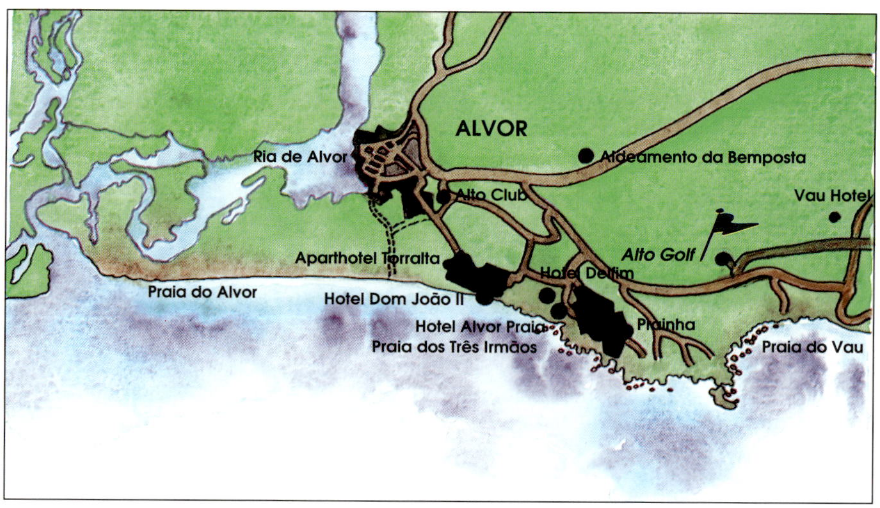

> *My philosophy when designing a golf course is that the course should be testing for low handicap players, but also provide an enjoyable game for the ordinary club player. Alto Golf meets these two criteria admirably.*
>
> Sir Henry Cotton

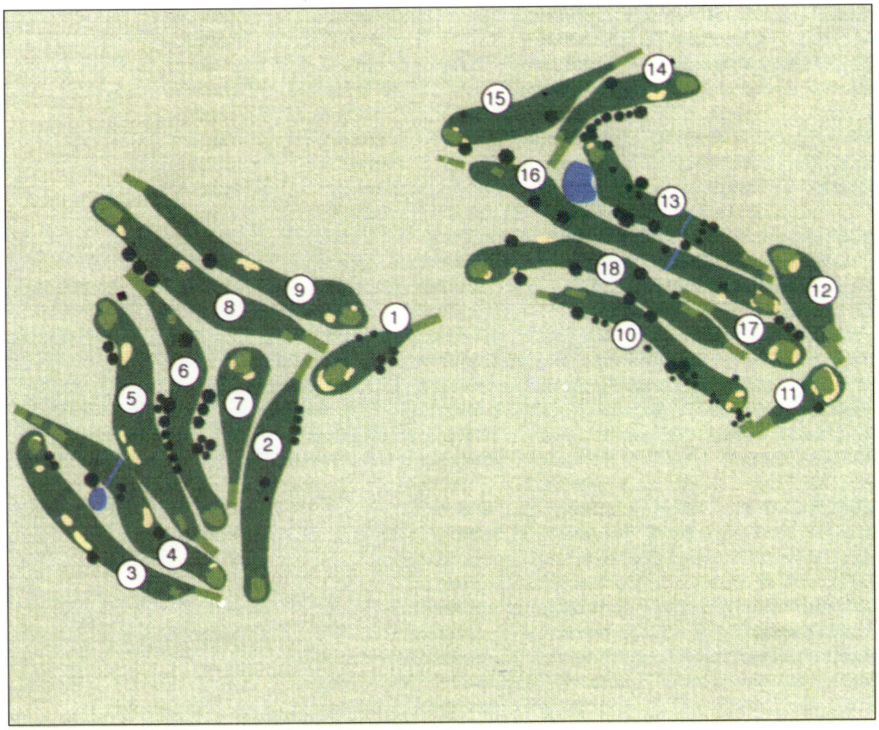

OTHER ATTRACTIONS

Alvor - *some good restaurants and small bars.*
Praia da Rocha - *many more restaurants and bars and one of the region's biggest beaches; small secluded coves nearby*
Portimão - *the nearest big town, second largest port in Algarve.*

	MENS								LADIES			
HOLE	W	Y	PAR	S.I.	A	B	C	D	R	PAR	S.I.	+/-
1	162	136	3	16					114	3	16	
2	364	348	4	5					332	4	5	
3	419	403	5	9					339	5	9	
4	400	321	4	2					304	4	2	
5	437	427	5	7					387	5	7	
6	401	377	4	1					358	4	1	
7	201	188	3	13					177	3	13	
8	323	293	4	17					258	4	17	
9	376	362	4	11					348	4	11	
OUT	3083	2855	36						2617	36		

MARKERS SIGNATURE

PLAYERS SIGNATURE

	MENS								LADIES			
HOLE	W	Y	PAR	S.I.	A	B	C	D	R	PAR	S.I.	+/-
10	410	351	4	4					329	4	4	
11	152	120	3	14					108	3	14	
12	136	124	3	18					106	3	18	
13	416	402	5	8					373	5	8	
14	262	[illegible]	4	13					233	4	16	
15	370	361	4	10					340	4	10	
16	604	589	5	3					530	5	3	
17	160	124	3	12					104	3	12	
18	532	510	5	6					493	5	6	
IN	3042	2828	36						2616	36		
OUT	3083	2855	36						2617	36		
T	6125	5683	72						5233	72		
				STROKES RECEIVED					STROKES RECEIVED			
				NET SCORE					NET SCORE			

PENINA

Maestro's masterpiece

The Championship course is the late Sir Henry Cotton's masterpiece and the course by which he wished to be remembered. He was the first to foresee the high potential for golf in the Algarve. The opening of Penina triggered the region's golf boom.

Sir Henry, who passed away in 1987 at the age of 80, was buried at his request at the nearby village of Mexilhoeira Grande.

There are many interesting stories about the years he spent in residence at Penina. Perhaps the best known concerns the donkey called 'Pacífico' which he trained as a caddie to carry two golf bags around the course. The animal was bought impulsively after a chicken barbecue meal in the nearby Monchique hills.

Unlike the vast majority of Algarve courses, Penina is a flat, parkland type course, having been built on former rice

*Page 150-1:
12th green across
Turtle Creek*

*A typically well
defended Penina green*

*Flashback: Henry
Cotton and 'Pacífico'.
On the right is Penina
pro Robin Liddle in
more youthful days*

9th green with hotel in background

paddies and scrubland. Most of the drainage ditches in the paddies were retained and partially modified into tricky water hazards, but the dramatic change of terrain was helped by the planting of about 250,000 trees which now line most of the fairways.

However, golf course construction methods and irrigation equipment have changed considerably since the mid-sixties. In early 1994 the course owners decided to upgrade the entire layout. The course was therefore closed for twelve months as from September 1994.

During this period, golfers who are guests at the hotel have the choice of playing on the 9-hole Resort course and several 18-hole courses in the region with which special arrangements have been made.

Cotton's original championship layout is naturally being conserved, but improved drainage will avoid the heavy conditions which were occasionally encountered during autumn and winter rains. The famous long tees allow for widely varying hole lengths to be played.

The course opens with two testing par 4's, the first being a long dog-leg to the

Opposite page: Bird's-eye view of Penina Hotel

left. The second, which is stroke index 1, includes an out-of-bounds water hazard all the way down the left-hand side. Only a long, well-placed drive will entice you to go for the long carry over the water which crosses the fairway just short of the green. Most players are forced to play safe before the hazard and depend on approaching close enough to hole out with a single putt to score par on this excellent hole.

The one and only par 5 on the front nine, the fifth, is an interesting dog-leg. The line from the tee is towards two bunkers just before a long water hazard which crosses the fairway at about 45 degrees from

Opposite page upper: Parkland leading to 18th green

Opposite page lower: Par 4 7th

Mobile bar

right to left. Conventionally, the second shot is played over the canal to a large expanse of fairway on the right. From there the approach shot must cross back over the canal to a raised, sloping green. Adventurous golfers can, however, attempt to draw their second shot left of the water. By dodging trees and rough on the left as well as two bunkers close to the green, a birdie chance can be set up.

On the ninth, a difficult par 4 dog-leg to the left, the drive should be at least 200 metres long to open up the line to the green which has the majestic Penina hotel as a backdrop. You must negotiate three

11th fairway foliage

bunkers guarding the front of the narrow two-tier green on the approach shot to make par or better.

The outward nine is par 35, but coming back we have four par 5's (strangely enough the tenth, eleventh, seventeenth and eighteenth) giving a total par of 38 for the back nine. The twelfth and thirteenth are good tests of golf, the former being a 397-metre straight par 4 with a narrow tree-lined fairway and an excellent view of the Monchique hills in the background. The approach over a water hazard to the green demands steady nerves.

13th fairway

Like the three other par 3's at this course, the thirteenth is long and at 208 metres requires a long iron or a wood shot. The slightly elevated green is protected by bunkers on either side but the main danger, at least for slicers, is the right-hand lake extending from tee to green. Many a good score has been ruined here, so a par is a bonus.

The sixteenth is another tough par

3, albeit with a less dangerous water hazard. The two finishing par 5's are not too long at 450 metres each and both capable of being birdied.

For those who know the Penina championship course it will be interesting to re-discover its charms at the end of 1995 after its £2 million face-lift.

Don't disregard the 9-hole Resort course. There are some stiff holes, such as the 362- metre par 4 sixth where the drive must be fired through a narrow avenue of towering trees with an out-of-bounds area to the right. The following hole is a tricky dog-leg left par 4 with water coming into play on the right near the green. Hole number eight is a long par 3 (202 metres) with several bunkers ready to trap errant shots. Not many birdies are seen here.

The Academy course offers a relaxing round of 9 holes for beginners, or a test of one's short game. The narrow fairways and small greens put a premium on accuracy.

Three opening holes on Resort course

COURSE INFORMATION

OWNED BY: *Forte Hotels, P.O. Box 146, 8502 Portimão Codex, Tel: (082) 415415 Fax: (082) 415000*

GOLF DIRECTOR: *Leonel Rio*
PROS: *Robin Liddle, José Lourenço and José Marcelino.*

COURSE ARCHITECT: *Sir Henry Cotton*

FOUNDED: *1966*

Nº. OF HOLES:
18 - Championship course.
Par (SSS): 73 (73)
9 - Resort (formerly Monchique). Par: 35
9 - Academy (formerly Quinta) course.
Par: 30

LENGTHS IN METRES: *Championship 6,439; Resort 2,987; Academy 2,035.*

LAST IMPORTANT TOURNAMENT: *1993 TAP (Air Portugal) Amateur Open*

GREEN FEES: *No charge for hotel guests. Visitors: 18 holes Championship course - closed until Sept. 1995. 18 holes Resort course - 6,000$ 18 holes Academy course - closed until Sept. 1995 18 holes on the Championship and Resort courses during June, July and August, between 11.00 a.m. and 3.00 p.m., are charged at half price.*

REQUIREMENTS TO PLAY AS A VISITOR: *handicaps (Men 28, Ladies 36) on main courses.*

AMENITIES

Pro shop
Driving range: 50 balls - 750$
100 balls - 1,500$
Putting-green
Chipping green
Swing analysis laboratory
Lessons: One hour - 8,000$
half hour - 4,000$
Club hire: 18 holes - 4,000$
per week - 24,000$
Trolleys: per day - 800$
per week 4,800$
Buggies: 9 holes - 3,000$
18 holes - 5,400$

CLUBHOUSE: *Located in the 5-star hotel; open to visitors. Includes changing rooms, pro shop with reception desk, equipment storage in addition to bar and snack service.*

Championship

MENS S.S.S. 73											LADIES S.S.S. 73		
HOLE	MARKER	WHITE	YELLOW	PAR	S.I.			WON LOST POINTS			RED	PAR	S.I.
1		411	392	4	6						363	4	6
2		401	384	4	1						331	4	1
3		301	286	4	12						264	4	12
4		375	359	4	5						288	4	5
5		463	443	5	10						393	5	10
6		186	164	3	18						137	3	18
7		299	254	4	14						216	4	14
8		180	166	3	17						127	3	17
9		405	379	4	3						318	4	3
OUT		3021	2827	35							2437	35	

HOLE	MARKER	WHITE	YELLOW	PAR	S.I.						RED	PAR	S.I.
10		500	482	5	7						464	5	7
11		491	474	5	9						430	5	9
12		397	375	4	2						330	4	2
13		208	171	3	13						155	3	13
14		394	375	4	4						331	4	4
15		318	302	4	15						265	4	15
16		210	176	3	16						135	3	16
17		450	437	5	8						380	5	8
18		450	435	5	11						395	5	11
IN		3418	3227	38							2885	38	
OUT		3021	2827	35							2437	35	
Total		6439	6054	73							5322	73	
		HANDICAP											
		NETT/RESULT											

Note the interesting old photographs and illustrations of Henry Cotton in the clubhouse.

CATERING: *5-star hotel bars and restaurants. Mobile bar on course.*

OTHER ATTRACTIONS

Alvor - *a fishing village with small restaurants and a beach;*

Portimão - *the Algarve's second largest town, a fishing port with plenty of shops;*

Praia da Rocha - *a bustling seaside resort with a huge beach;*

Monchique - *in the wooded range of hills of the same name, is a pleasant drive away.*

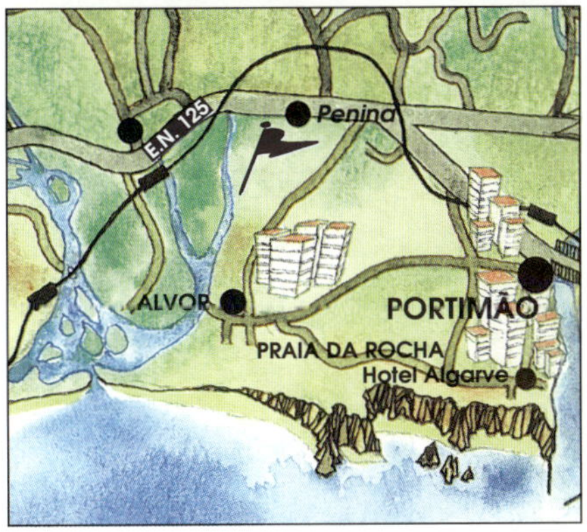

HOW TO FIND: *5 km west of Portimão on the EN.125 road, less than 1 km after the turn-off to Alvor.*

❛ Penina is one of the finest golf set-ups there is anywhere.❜

Sir Henry Cotton.

❛ In Forte's continuous pursuit of quality, the Penina Golf and Resort Hotel has embarked on a major project that will upgrade all of its 36 holes to rank as Europe's finest golf resort. ❜

Andrew White, former Director of Golf.

Resort

MENS S.S.S. 70										LADIES S.S.S. 70		
HOLE	WHITE	YELLOW	PAR	S.I.			WON LOST POINTS			RED	PAR	S.I.
1	391	372	4	4						332	4	4
2	349	337	4	8						324	4	8
3	329	306	4	14						297	4	14
4	140	129	3	18						123	3	18
5	499	484	5	10						461	5	10
6	362	352	4	2						323	4	2
7	294	279	4	16						252	4	16
8	202	180	3	12						160	3	12
9	421	403	4	6						358	4	6
OUT	2987	2842	35							2630	35	

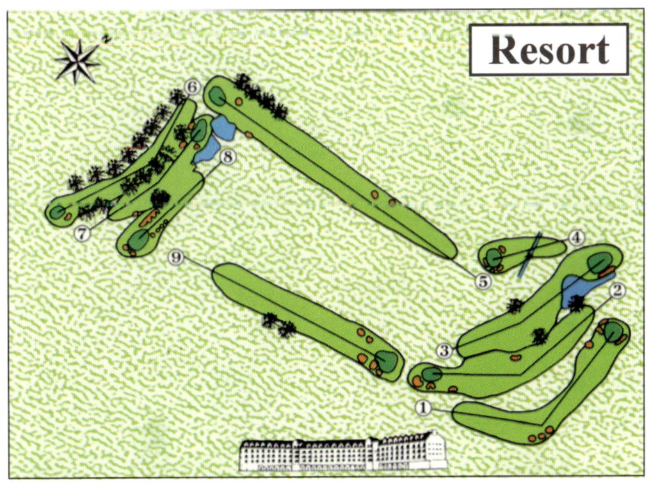

PALMARES

Unforgettable,

Page 162-3: View from putting green

Opposite page: Short 4th

Left: 18th fairway in early February

Below: Clubhouse grounds

especially in almond blossom time

Palmares, an interesting course, is best known for its breathtaking scenery. The setting is idyllic, with the majority of the holes on gentle slopes above the extensive beach stretching from the new Lagos marina to the mouth of the Alvor River.

Course architect Frank Pennink took full advantage of the magnificent site and, in passing, threw in a sequence of five pure links holes between the railway and the beach, evoking memories of famous British layouts.

The upper holes wind through groves of almond and fig trees and the course is renowned for its annual Almond Blossom tournament week in February. It is then that the trees, covered in a mass of pink and white bloom, create an unforgettable sight.

Ideally, you need a drive of at least 230 metres, ending up left of centre on the downhill first fairway, to have a view of the green further down and to the right. It is defended in front by two bunkers. This is a tricky par 4 opener at 418 metres off the championship tee.

Immediately after are the links holes. The most challenging hole on the whole course is the 550-metre fifth with a narrow fairway which runs parallel to the beach. If you are able to keep out of the dunes on either side, the third shot can be played over trees direct to the raised green tucked in to the right. Playing more conservatively, you will normally need to count on a single putt to extract a well earned par on this monster hole.

The sixth is a nerve-tingling short par 4 with a 90 degree dog-leg right which tempts long hitters to go for the green or the adjacent fairway over an large, threatening expanse of mainly dry, reed and scrub-filled inlet, a lateral salt-water hazard.

Opposite page: 5th links hole

Below: 4th green

Heading up the inclines again we later come to the attractive 165-metre par 3 tenth played over a large dip to a green at the top of a steep slope. Anything short will normally roll back down, and bunkers guard the left-hand side of the large, split-level green. The view from this green towards the historic town of Lagos and its wide bay is truly spectacular.

The back nine, however, is memorable for two tough par 4 holes, the twelfth and sixteenth. The former is a full 400 metres from the back tee with a fairway which curves gradually left, demanding two long shots to the double-tiered green with a narrow entrance between bunkers.

Hole sixteen is even longer at 418

Opposite page left:
8th hole

Opposite page right: view over clubhouse to Alvor estuary

Left: 1st green

Below: 17th green

metres with an uphill target area for the drive. The fairway dog-legs right and once over the hill it slopes severely left down to the trees and an out-of-bounds area. Birdies on these two holes are rarities and pars more than welcome.

Palmares cannot be described without mentioning the attractive par 5, dog-leg left seventeenth. As the stroke index 16 suggests, it is not difficult. The scenery is outstanding with a panoramic view of the Atlantic, the Alvor estuary and the coastline beyond. The second shot can be played across the left-hand rough and easily reach the green. Take care of the large trees at the corner which must be cleared, especially when playing from the sloping fairway.

COURSE INFORMATION

OWNED BY:
Palmares Investimentos e Urbanizações, Lda.
Apartado 74, Palmares,
Meia Praia, 8600 Lagos.
Tel: (082) 762953/61
Fax: (082) 762534

GOLF DIRECTOR: *Francisco Cabral*
SECRETARY: *Dennis Garvey*
PRO'S: *Luís Espadinha, José Dias*

COURSE ARCHITECT: *Frank Pennink*

FOUNDED: *1975*

NO. OF HOLES: *18. Par (SSS): 71 (72)*

LENGTH IN METRES: *5,961*

GREEN FEES:
(effective Oct 1994 to May 31 1995)

	Single	*Married couple*
18 holes	*7,000$*	*14,000$*
9 holes	*4,000$*	*8,000$*
One week (a)	*33,000$*	*57,200$*
One month (a)	*77,000$*	*121,000$*
Annual	*44,000$ (b)*	*66,000$ (c)*

(a) Not applicable in month of March.
(b) Plus daily green fee of 2,500$ per 18-hole round, or 1,500$ per 9-hole round.
(c) Plus daily green fee of 3,600$ per 18-hole round (jointly) or 2,500$ for 18-hole round if playing as a single. 9 holes, 2,100$ (jointly) or 1,500$ if playing as a single. 50% discount for juniors (under 18).

REQUIREMENTS TO PLAY AS A VISITOR:
Current handicap certificate.

AMENITIES

Pro shop
Driving range: 50 balls - 500$
Putting greens
Chipping green
Lessons: one hour - 6.000$;
half hour - 3,000$
Club hire: 3,000$
Trolleys: manual - 500$; electric - 1,500$
Buggies: 5,000$

CLUBHOUSE: *Small but functional; well situated with beautiful view from the open verandah. Includes pro shop and catering facilities. Separate building with changing rooms.*

CATERING: *Bar and restaurant with snack and light meal service. No catering on the course.*

OTHER ATTRACTIONS

Lagos - *a historic town which played an important role in Henry the Navigator's exploits in the 15th century. Now a lively tourist town with plenty of good restaurants.*
Beaches - *a choice to the south and west of the town.*

HOW TO FIND: *5 km east of Lagos. Follow "Meia Praia" and "Golf" road signs near the marina at the eastern outskirts of Lagos on the EN125 main road to Portimão. Take care at the two railway level-crossings on the way. An alternative route from the EN125 is south from the village of Odiáxere. Part of the road is rough and unpaved and it is not recommended in wet weather.*

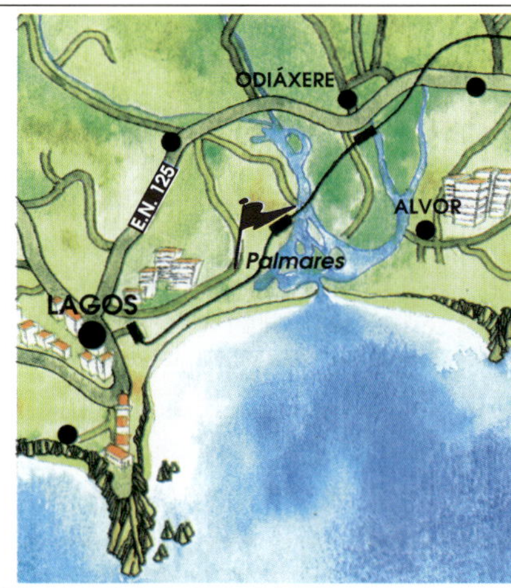

"Palmares is one of the gems of European golf. It is not a lavish club, but one glorious in its unpretentiousness. There are many who would happily sit high up on the clubhouse veranda and simply admire the glorious view across the bay without venturing on to the golf course at all."

Malcolm Campbell, Golf Monthly.

No. Hole	DISTÂNCIAS METROS DISTANCE METRES Camp Champ	Homens Men	Senhoras Ladies	PAR	Pontos (STRK) Stroke Index
1	418	403	360	4	4
2	321	297	242	4	13
3	287	279	270	4	7
4	142	133	121	3	15
5	550	515	457	5	1
6	344	294	245	4	9
7	462	450	403	5	11
8	142	131	119	3	17
9	317	303	281	4	6
Ida Out	2983	2805	2498	36	
10	165	156	142	3	14
11	271	260	252	4	18
12	400	372	324	4	3
13	386	364	314	4	8
14	347	340	324	4	5
15	212	192	178	3	12
16	418	370	310	4	2
17	458	447	384	5	16
18	321	308	294	4	10
Volta In	2978	2809	2522	35	
TOTAL	5961	5614	5020	71	

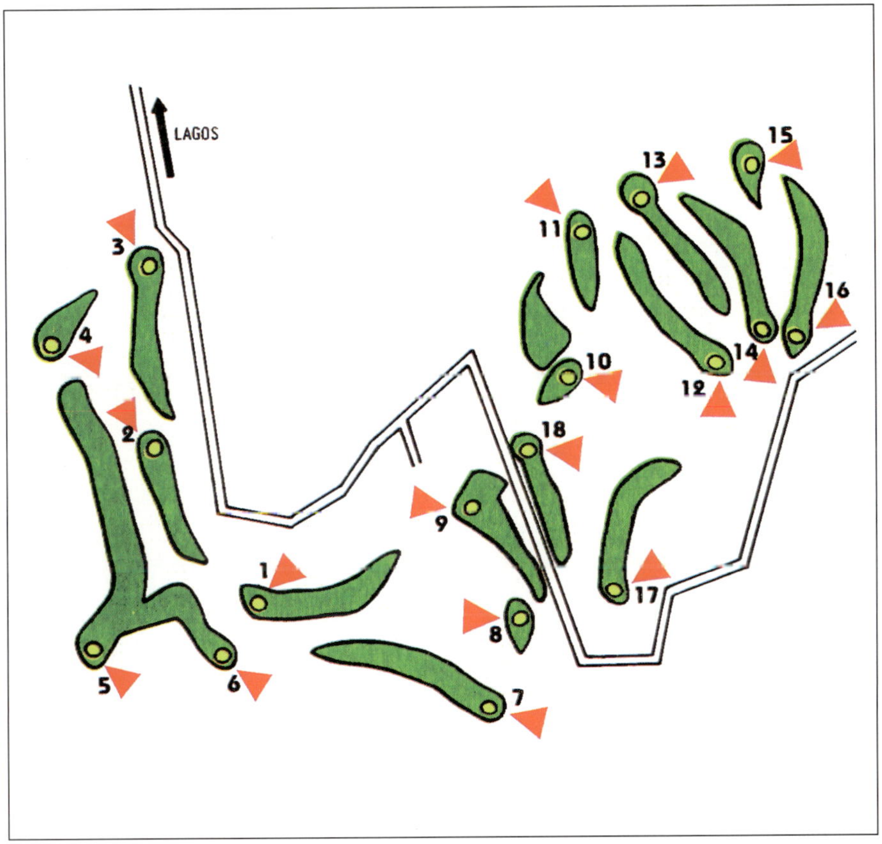

Parque da Floresta

Unique challenges await in western hills

Parque da Floresta is located amongst rolling, hilly terrain near the south-western tip of Portugal, the "Land's End" of Continental Europe. The layout, designed by former Spanish amateur champion Pepe Gancedo, architect of the well-known Torrequebrada course near Málaga in Spain, was virtually carved out of the hills and many of the natural contours were retained.

Because of this, most of the holes, especially on the first nine, are testing if not somewhat daunting for the average

golfer. But this is what intrigues those who play it for the first time. The tendency is for golfers to go back time and again in an attempt to master the trickier holes. It is a case of the greater the challenge, the better the reward.

Unlike most courses, the controversial Parque da Floresta has an infinite variety of holes, each one with individual character. A combination of finesse and long precise shots is essential to score well.

The owners, who acquired the complex at the end of 1993, have embarked on a programme of continuous course improvement. Particular attention is being given to hazardous areas where an unlucky bounce or roll could lead to an unplayable lie, lost ball or an out-of-bounds situation.

One could mention several notable holes. The most memorable start with the first, a 513 - metre par 5. It bends gradually left along a fairway sloping down from the right. A tee more to the left and a wider landing area for the tee-shot have been built. Longer hitters can choose to aim their second shot straight for the green over a deep

Opposite page: Ravine at the 15th

P.172-3: Short 5th

chasm. This hole, incidentally, went into the Algarve history books as one of the very few where an albatross has been scored. Derek Young, owner of a property on the Parque da Floresta development, achieved this feat in 1993 with a drive and four-iron shot.

The short fifth, a mere 110 metres from the back tee, with its smallish green on the crown of a hillock well below the level of the tee, is a real test of nerves even when the wind drops.

At 525 metres, the ninth is the longest hole and stroke index 1. With the green perched at the top of a steep slope up from

Opposite page: View from behind 9th green

Left: 10th fairway

Above: Water guards 16th green

Right: Clubhouse from 17th fairway

Opposite page: Almost home - 18th fairway

a stream which crosses the fairway, nothing much is to be gained from clearing the water hazard on the second shot. An accurately lofted approach to the plateau green is needed to par or birdie this tough hole before you climb further towards the clubhouse and the tenth tee.

The opening hole on the back nine is a more benign par 5, and immediately after it there is an attractive 148-metre par 3 with a lake to the left and back of the green. The greenside bunker on the left often prevents balls from finding a worse fate in the watery grave.

Two long straight shots are required on the 400-metre twelfth up a valley to an elevated green. Anything short and right will tend to roll down the slopes, leaving a difficult pitch shot.

Although the homeward stretch is generally less severe than most holes on the first nine, players must still contend with the sloping, undulating fairway of the par 5 fourteenth. Plenty of trouble with rough and out-of-bounds on the right here - then the terraced green is long and narrow, demanding a delicate approach shot.

Parque da Floresta's best known par 3 is the scenic fifteenth which demands a 159-metre stroke over a tree-filled ravine across which is a large wooden bridge. The sloping, split level green is one of the trickiest on the course and a birdie here is highly satisfactory.

Hundreds of palm-trees of types adapted to the local micro-climate are being planted around the course to blend into the attractive surroundings.

COURSE INFORMATION

OWNED BY: *E. F. & F. Lda. through Golfe Santo António Lda., Vale do Poço, Budens, 8650 Vila do Bispo. Tel: (082) 65333, 65341 Fax: (082) 65157*

GOLF DIRECTOR: *Bernard Murphy*
PRO: *Peter Dolan*

COURSE ARCHITECT: *Pepe Gancedo*

FOUNDED: *1987*

Nº. OF HOLES: *18. Par (SSS): 72 (72)*

LENGTH IN METRES: *5,875*

GREEN FEES: *Daily - Esc: 6,000$; weekly - 30,000$; monthly - 72,000$; annually - 150,000$. Reduced fees for juniors; discounts for those staying at the self-catering accommodation available next to the course.*

REQUIREMENTS TO PLAY AS A VISITOR: *None*

AMENITIES

Pro shop		
Driving range:	*50 balls*	*500$*
	100 balls	*1,000$*
Putting green		
Chipping green		
Lessons		
Club hire:		*2,000$*
Trolleys:	*18 holes*	*500$*
Buggies:	*18 holes*	*4,500$*
	9 holes	*3,000$*

CLUBHOUSE: *Attractive and spacious permanent building with all conveniences. Large first-floor verandah with panoramic view over about half of the course, and the Atlantic Ocean in the distance.*

CATERING: *Good restaurant and bar service on the clubhouse premises.*

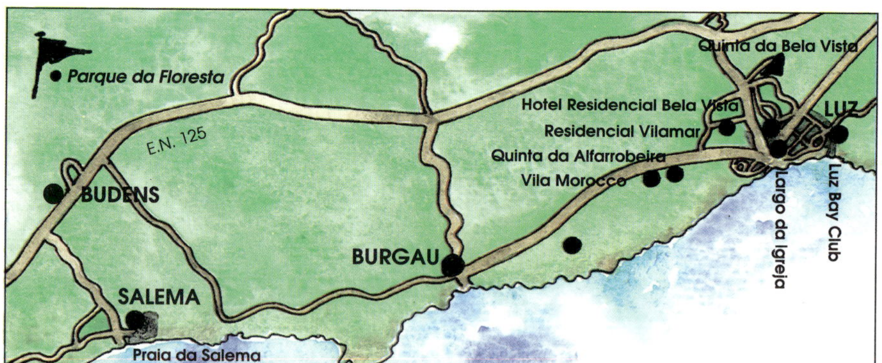

HOW TO FIND: *Just over 1 km west of the village of Budens, 16 km west of Lagos; signposted on the right of the EN125 main road.*

> *Pepe Gancedo is the Pablo Picasso of golf course architecture. He is essentially an artist, as all architects should be, and Parque Floresta is unquestionably an artistic masterpiece. It offers the golfing experience of a lifetime.*
>
> Peter Dobereiner, golf writer.

Hole	Distance in Metres			Par	S.I.
1	493	438	421	5	5
2	341	326	310	4	12
3	157	143	123	3	16
4	446	415	379	5	3
5	112	88	69	3	18
6	358	314	255	4	8
7	180	141	113	3	10
8	292	281	270	4	14
9	485	452	352	5	1
Out	2864	2598	2292	36	

Hole	Distance in Metres			Par	S.I.
10	440	426	376	5	15
11	139	143	110	3	11
12	368	318	262	4	2
13	351	333	323	4	7
14	512	491	409	5	4
15	148	144	112	3	9
16	271	234	215	4	17
17	367	340	301	4	6
18	327	297	255	4	13
In	2923	2726	2363	36	

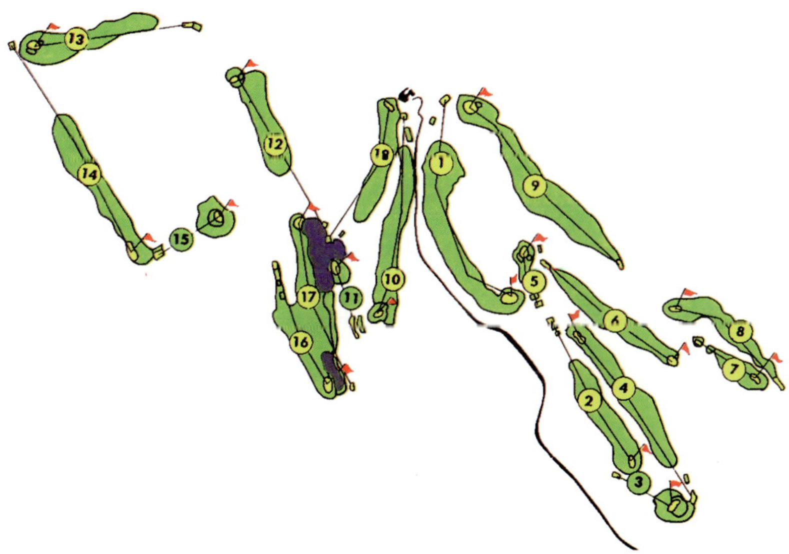

OTHER ATTRACTIONS

Lagos - *bustling tourist town of historic interest;*
Salema, Burgau and Praia da Luz - *peaceful fishing villages each with a beach, restaurants and bars.*
West coast - *many spectacular, nearly deserted beaches.*
Sagres - *fortress and rugged cliff scenery.*
Cape St. Vincent - *lighthouse at land's end.*

At ease

Below: Praia da Luz

There is plenty to do in the Algarve besides play golf. Golf widows and their families, as well as players who want to take a break from the courses, will find that Portugal's most southerly province is a fascinating place which warmly invites exploration.

Drive and walk along the coast, through the villages and towns, the farmlands and countryside, and up into the wooded hillsides to discover just how enchanting the Algarve is. It is unlike any other place you have ever been.

Beautiful bodies galore are to be found on the most popular south coast

Incoming tide

beaches in summer, but for more private sunbathing and swimming there are scores of secluded coves to be sought out. If you fancy a stroll along a beach on balmy summer evenings or mild days in winter, spring and autumn, you may have miles of golden sand to yourself. On the undeveloped west coast, from Sagres northwards, there are breathtaking beaches which are almost deserted all year round.

Water-skiing can be arranged at many resorts. Vilamoura and Lagos are the main sailing centres. The safest conditions for windsurfing are within the sheltered lagoons of the eastern Algarve and inside

Dona Ana beach, near Lagos

Above: *Inshore stacks*

Right: *Offshore sails*

Opposite page
Top: Vilamoura marina

Bottom: Cape St Vincent

the breakwaters of the river Arade. Surfing conditions are generally best on south-western beaches. The Algarve's clear inshore waters in the rockier western half of the south coast are ideal for snorkeling and scuba diving because of the abundance of colourful marine life and sunken shipwrecks.

Record-sized marlin of more than 1,000 pounds have been caught about 20 miles offshore, but game fishing boats based in Vilamoura and Portimão mostly catch blue sharks and tuna. A mecca for anglers with long rods, plenty of line and a head for heights are the cliffs at Sagres where, if conditions are right, the turbulent waters teem with sea bass and bream.

There are exhilarating walks along clifftop paths past blowhole vents, caverns, rock arches and stacks - all products of natural erosion. For a different perspective, take a boat trip along the base of these fantastically fashioned cliffs, and take along your camera.

The clarity of light in the Algarve makes it a special place for photographers. There are plenty of picturesque subjects inland as well as along the coast. The narrow cobbled streets and older architecture in towns and villages often present pleasing shapes and stark light and shade contrasts which are much more photogenic than anything produced in the second half of the 20th century.

At the entrances to churches look out for columns resembling twisted ropes, or stone motifs with a nautical or natural

theme. These are examples of Manueline ornamentation of the late Gothic period, which celebrated Portugal's sea-going successes beginning with the discoveries instigated by Prince Henry the Navigator and his captains Bartolomeu Dias and Vasco da Gama.

The Algarve is steeped in history. Lagos was where Prince Henry had his caravels built and victualled in the 15th century. Silves was the scene of many medieval battles as Crusaders from northern Europe joined the Portuguese to expel the Muslim Moors who occupied southern Portugal from the 8th to the 13th centuries. Right in the heart of Vilamoura and also near Estói there are Roman ruins. At Alcalar and other more remote parts of the Algarve there are standing stones erected by Neolithic people 5,000 years ago.

Loulé, with its medieval walls, is the largest of the Algarve's inland towns. An easy drive from many of the golf courses, it is renowned as a crafts centre. On walking around its narrow streets in the vicinity of its arabesque market, you may catch glimpses of coppersmiths, saddlers, basket weavers and cabinet makers at work.

In all Algarve towns the municipal market is a centre of colourful and

garrulous activity each morning. It is still the best and cheapest shopping place for fresh foodstuffs. A wide variety of fish, meat, vegetables and fruit, all wholesome, freshly caught or home-grown, are sold under one roof.

The variety of seafood on sale in these markets is amazing and this is reflected on restaurant menus. Most of the restaurants in the vicinity of the golf courses serve well prepared international dishes. If you get a chance, though, try some typically Portuguese dishes such as caldo verde (shredded cabbage soup), caldeirada de peixe (fish stew), lulas recheadas (stuffed squid) or bacalhau, salted cod, the nearest thing to a national dish for which there are

Above: Seafood sample

Right: Beached fishing boats

Opposite page Top: Tavira water-front

Left: Piety and palms

Right: Village life

said to be recipes for every day of the year.

Portugal is, of course, a wine country and its seafood or chicken dishes are nicely complemented by vinho verde, a light, slightly bubbly wine from the north-west of the country, or by whites from the famous Dão region in north-central Portugal. Wine connoisseurs will perhaps appreciate best of all the reds, such as those from the Dão, Bairrada and Douro regions. It is the Douro valley in the north of Portugal which produces the port wine so beloved in northern Europe but, strangely, not much consumed in Portugal itself.

More commercially important than vines in the Algarve is citrus production. With the introduction of modern methods

Above:
Vine-shaded view

Right:
Monchique hills

Left: Terraced hillside

Below: Almond blossom

Above: Hoopoe

of irrigation, oranges have become the most important crop. The most prolific citrus picking season roughly coincides with the main golfing season. January and more especially February are the almond blossom months when great swaths of gently sloping hillsides are covered with white and pink petals. From then until late June there is a riot of natural colour in the countryside. Oleander, mimosa, Judas trees, jacaranda, broom, gum cistus, orchids and many other blooms and wildflowers vie for the eye.

For the birdwatcher there is a dazzling variety of resident species as well as seasonal visitors and passage migrants. One of the most dazzling, the hoopoe, with its pink plumage and boldly barred black and white wings, is particularly fond of feeding on fairways. The lakes of the San Lorenzo course are a haven for the rare purple gallinule. But go to the wetlands of Castro Marim in the extreme east to see storks, black-winged stilts and flamingos, or to Cape St. Vincent in the extreme west to look for migrating seabirds.

Wherever you go, whatever you do, try to take your time about it. Nothing worthwhile happens in a hurry here.

** This chapter is adapted from the book* ***Get to Know the Algarve***

Services & Facilities

This section comprises selected advertisers, arranged by area. It is followed by an A-Z list of useful information.

GOLF PAR EXCELLENCE

The largest golf resort in Europe, Quinta do Lago, is just over two hours flying time from most continental capitals, which means that you can leave home in the morning and be enjoying a pleasant game of golf in the year-round Algarvean sunshine in the afternoon.

Understanding the golfer's need for quality services, luxury accommodation with professional teaching clinics is provided for individuals and groups on long weekends or vacations, as well as other sporting facilities and a host of bars and restaurants for a convivial nightlife.

Host to the Portuguese Open seven times, Quinta do Lago's 72 holes of golf offer several championship combinations to test all levels of skill, and the breath-taking scenery enhances the sheer pleasure of the golfing experience.

Indeed, many of our fine properties bordering the courses are purchased by keen golfers with the right to life-time golf club membership. (Those who are so tempted by the Quinta do Lago way of life that they can't keep away!)

For further information, please contact:
Planal S.A., Quinta do Lago, 8135 Almancil, Algarve, Portugal. Tel. 089 394270/3 Fax. 089 394936

EUROPE'S LARGEST GOLF RESORT MILES OF CLEAN, GOLDEN BEACH - PEACE - TRANQUILITY
PART OF UNESCO-PROTECTED RIA FORMOSA - EXCLUSIVE PROPERTIES WITH GOLF, LAKES AND SEA VIEWS
MATURE, PROVEN INVESTMENT - SOPHISTICATED SOCIAL LIFE - HORSERIDING - TENNIS - WATERSPORTS

Four Seasons
Vilamoura
Want a share of the action?

Four Seasons Vilamoura is a prestigious holiday base for those who play golf, and an idyllic oasis for those who don't.

Completely surrounded by the ninth and tenth fairways of one championship course and in the heartland of two more, this is a place devoted to all-year-round peace and pleasure amid cascading waters, palm trees and scented gardens.

Stylish studio,one and two bedroom apartments form a three-storey crescent on the edge of the fairways. They envelop a leisure sanctuary of arched patios, sun-terraces, exotic plants and huge swimming pools.

The focal point is an elegant clubhouse which encompasses a sumptuous lounge, restaurant, bar, snooker room, winter garden, heated swimming pool, air-conditioned squash court, gymnasium, beauty salon, sauna, jacuzzi........

Come to think of it, jacuzzi baths are everywhere at Four Seasons Vilamoura. They are in all of the apartments, as are fitted wardrobes, custom-designed French furniture, Italian marble dining tables, 'fridges with separate freezers, micro-waves as well as convectional ovens, washing machines and clothes dryers.

Needless-to-say, this sort of pampered holiday lifestyle is exclusive, available only to members and their guests. There are currently nearly 3,000 members, each a "clubshare" owner holding a legally watertight right to annually use a Four Seasons Vilamoura apartment and all of the club's facilities for the rest of their lives.

Opposite page: Four Seasons serenity

Left: Poolside relaxation

Below: The comforts of indoor fun

The maximum number of owners who will be admitted to this convivial and cosmopolitan club is estimated to be 4,150.

All visitors to the Algarve are welcome to go to Four Seasons Vilamoura, spend the day there free of charge as guests and see the set-up for themselves.

Becoming a member is not quite as easy as ambling over to the 1st tee with a Four Seasons Vilamoura guaranteed starting time and at least a 25% discount off the green fee, but it is worth considering - especially if you want to keep the non-golfing members of your family happy.

Sheraton
ALGARVE

PINE CLIFFS

ITT SHERATON LUXURY COLLECTION

PRAIA DA FALÉSIA, APARTADO 644, 8200 ALBUFEIRA, PORTUGAL.
TEL: (351) 89 501999 - FAX: (351) 89 501950 - TELEX: 58524

O LITORAL

Restaurante & Grill

Dagmar & António Marotta

Value & Taste
in delightful fishing village

Established over 7 years ago, this restaurant offers the perfect combination of Portuguese cuisine tailored for more sophisticated tastes. The house speciality is plaice which, if you wish, is filletted at your table, and a traditional roast meat is usually available with fresh vegetables of the day. Prices are very reasonable, as is witnessed by the many foreign residents you'll always see eating there both summer and winter. Set in the delightful village of Benagil, only 10 minutes from Carvoeiro.

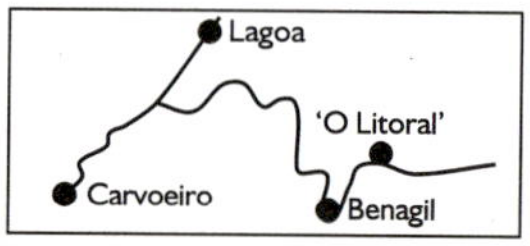

Tel: (082) 359649 Benagil - 8400 LAGOA

QUINTA DA SAUDADE

Restaurant

Vale de Parra, Albufeira

Tel: (089) 591761

A short drive from Albufeira. Keith and Louise invite you to join them in their beautiful country restaurant and bar, warmed by open log fires. Enjoy their delicious home-made cuisine in comfort. Separate full vegetarian and children's menu.

Within 2km of Salgados Golf Course.

Winter : Fri-Sat, 12.00-2.00pm, 7.00pm onwards.
Sunday : Traditional Roast Lunch, 12.00-3.00pm.
Summer : Tues-Sun, Bar snacks 12.00-3.00pm
Dinner, 7.00pm onwards.
Closed Mondays.

HOTEL ALMANSOR ★★★★

Resort, Conference & Golf Hotel
Carvoeiro / Algarve

Built on the rocks above the Vale Covo beach, this hotel has 293 rooms, all with air conditioning, direct telephone, radio, satellite T.V., safe, mini-bar and 24 hour room service. It also offers two restaurants, a coffee shop, a tobacco shop, games room, swimming pool, health club, tennis courts and a putting green. At your disposal is our own Golf Course, "Salgados", 20 minutes from the hotel, with transfers. Close by are the Carvoeiro Golf Courses of "Gramacho" and "Vale da Pinta", a horse riding centre, and water sports.

almansor

Praia Vale Covo / Carvoeiro, 8400 Lagoa
Tel : (82) 358026 ; Fax : (82) 358770 ; Tx : 57194

ENJOY THE PLEASURES OF A HOME IN THE ALGARVE

When you own your own home at Rocha Brava, whatever you're looking for - quiet beaches, magnificient scenery, rest and relaxation or sport and activity - it can all be yours.

Set high above the Atlantic, near Carvoeiro, Rocha Brava is one of the Algarve's most breathtaking locations. Yet its appointed apartments and villas, in landscaped gardens with swimming pools, are surprisingly accessible, offering you a Tennis Centre- with resident professional - and golf close by.

To enjoy the pleasures of Rocha Brava through every glorious season, ring GB 0483 771203 (24 hours) or Portugal (0)82 358775 for our brochure and inspection visit details.

Freehold properties from £74,000

Four-owners scheme from £23,500

Prices correct at time of publication.

TRAFALGAR HOUSE EUROPE

THE NEXT DEVELOPMENT IN YOUR LIFESTYLE

CARVOEIRO GOLFE COUNTRY CLUBE

Two new golf courses, recently opened in Algarve, Portugal's southern-most province. QUINTA DO GRAMACHO, a unique double 9 hole course, and VALE DE PINTA, an 18 hole championship course.

For more information about freehold properties, our successful Four Owners Scheme, accommodation and golf, please contact or visit our sales office.

Tel : (351) 82 357266 Fax : 357725

Address : Apartado 24, P-8400 Lagoa

SECOND HOME - FIRST CHOICE

★ ★ ★ ★ ★

HOTEL ALGARVE

BEACH AND GOLF
PRAIA DA ROCHA

Hotel Algarve is situated on one of the Algarve's finest and most famous beaches, with nearly all bedrooms having balconies overlooking the sea. It is surrounded by the best golf clubs of the region.

Special Golf Terms

For the Golf enthusiast, we have arranged special terms for seven top golf courses, selected for their variety and interest......Alto Golf, Penina, Palmares, Vale de Pinta, Salgados, Vilamoura III and Parque da Floresta.

Golf Packages

From October to April, Energetic Golf Packages are available for 3, 5 or 7 days.

For reservations, please contact :
Praia da Rocha – 8500 Portimão – Algarve – Portugal.
Tel: 082 415001/9 – Fax: 082 415999 – Telex: 57347

AIRPORT

There is only one airport in the Algarve and it is an uncomplicated place. It consists of three floors. Arrivals and departures are at either end of the ground floor. In between are the airline and hire car desks.

There is a cafe and restaurant on the second floor and a bar on the third floor sun-terrace overlooking the tarmac.

Incoming visitors from EU countries are required to show their passport at immigration control, but there are no other formalities. Departing passengers are asked to check in two hours before flight time. Airport telephone: (089) 818281

BANKS AND CURRENCY

Normal banking hours are Monday to Friday 8.30am to 3.0pm. All banks, except the ones at Faro airport and the ferry terminal at Vila Real de St° António, are closed weekends and public holidays. Exchange rates are prominently displayed at most banks in all tourist areas.

The escudo is abbreviated to Esc or symbolised with the $ sign after the amount. Escudo notes come in denominations of 500$, 1,000$, 2,000$, 5,000$ and 10,000$. A thousand escudos is sometimes called a *conto*. Thus, five thousands escudos is five *contos*. Coins are for 1$, 2$50, 5$, 10$, 20$ 50$, 100$ and 200$. The amount after the $ sign refers to the almost worthless centavos of which there are 100 to the escudo.

BEACHES

All of the popular beaches have bar-restaurants opened at least from the beginning of June to the end of September, though closed in winter. The popular beaches are patrolled by lifeguards during the summer and there is a safety flag system as follow: Green flag - conditions suitable for bathing and swimming; Yellow flag - suitable for strong swimmers only; Red - dangerous to go into the water; chequered flag - lifeguards temporarily absent.

BOAT TRIPS

Half and full-day pleasure cruises along the Algarve's spectacular coast sail from Vilamoura, Portimão and Lagos. Short trips to view local cliff formations and sea caves operate from most resorts towns and village beaches from Vilamoura to Sagres. From Portimão, river cruises chug up to the ancient capital of Silves and back. Longer cruises starting from Vila Real de St° António explore the Guadiana river with Portugal on the west bank and the Spanish province of Andalusia on the east.

CAR HIRE

Rentals can be arranged when booking your holiday in your home country, upon arrival at Faro airport, in any of the hotels or at agencies in all the main tourist resorts in the Algarve. The stipulations are that you must be at least 21-years-old and have held a driving licence for at least one year. The hire price includes third party insurance. On top of the basic hire price you must pay a 16% government tax. Optional extras: collision damage waiver, theft insurance, personal insurance.

CRIME

Theft from cars, bag snatching and house break-ins are depressingly common in tourist areas though no worse than most other places in Europe. Take sensible security precautions with valuables. Report robberies to the nearest police (GNR) station. The police will issue you with a document which should be handed to your insurance company when making a claim.

DRIVING

Drive on the right. Always carry your driving licence, registration document and insurance papers with you in the car. Spot-checks by traffic police are common and failure to be able to produce any of the above documents will result in an on-the-spot fine.

EMERGENCIES

The free phone emergency number anywhere in Portugal for police, fire service or ambulance is 115. If possible, ask someone who speaks Portuguese to do the phoning for you.

The state hospitals in Faro, Portimão and Lagos are open 24 hours a day for emergencies. There are a number of English, German and Dutch-speaking doctors in private practice in the Algarve.

Most European countries have representatives in the Algarve for those who need consular help.

GUIDEBOOKS & MAPS

Get to Know the Algarve by Len Port is the most comprehensive and readable book available on Portugal's southern province. It describes the Algarve's history, culture, customs, lifestyle and wildlife. Reference sections contain masses of practical information and suggestions about where to go and what to do.

Portugal's Pousada Route by Stuart Ross is a complete guide to the unique pousada hotel network. All of the pousadas and the areas around them are described in detail. It is a must for anyone touring Portugal who wants to stay in comfort and style.

Both these books are well illustrated and are available in German editions.

The *Insider's Tourist Map of Algarve* by illustrator Ana Ferreira is a fresh, clear and colourful aid to finding your way around the region. It includes new roads built in recent years. Sections of the map have been used with the "How to find" information in this book.

MUSEUMS

In Faro there are three: archaeology, regional ethnology and maritime museums. There are also small museums in Lagos, Silves, Albufeira, Moncarapacho, São Brás de Alportel, Tavira and Vila Real de Stº António.

NEWSPAPERS

Foreign newspapers are on sale at newsagents in all the main tourist areas, but a day after publication.

POSTAL SERVICES

Post offices are generally open from 8.30am to 6.0pm on weekdays, closed weekends. In small towns and villages they close for lunch. Allow up to 10 days for a letter or card to reach northern Europe addresses.

PUBLIC HOLIDAYS

All banks and post offices and many businesses close on the following national holidays: January 1, Good Friday, May 1, Corpus Christi, June 10, August 15, October 5, November 1, December 1, December 8, December 25. They also close locally on holidays celebrating local patron saint's days.

TAXIS

Traditionally, metered taxis in Portugal have been black with green roofs, but all new taxis have to conform to European Union cream. Fares from Faro airport to all the main resorts are at a set rate. There are taxi ranks in the centre of all the main towns and radio taxis are easily contacted.

TELEPHONING

The 089 area code takes in all phones between Faro and Albufeira, including the golf courses from Quinta do Lago to Salgados.

The 082 area code applies from Armação de Pera to Sagres and the courses Vale do Milho to Parque da Floresta.

081 is the eastern Algarve.

To ring the UK first dial 0044, then the area code minus the first zero, followed by the subscriber's number. To ring Portugal first dial 010 351.

TOURIST INFORMATION

The regional tourist board has offices in all the main tourist towns. Look out for a sign with the word *Turismo*. All information and leaflets are free.

You will find most hotel and resort receptionists very helpful.

Lucienne Erville - Marcel Marlier

Follet le petit chat

casterman

MARLIER

Le petit chat Follet rêve,
couché sur les pierres chaudes de la cour.
Bzz, Bzz ! Une mouche va, vient, repart.
Follet essaye de l'attraper,
mais la mouche a déjà disparu au loin.

Follet aimerait découvrir ce qu'il y a derrière le mur.
Il trouve une échelle et grimpe prudemment.
« Comme c'est haut !» soupire le petit chat.

Follet découvre alors un magnifique jardin.
Impatient, il saute sans regarder où il va.

Patatras

Dans sa chute, il a froissé trois capucines.

– Pardon, dit-il aux fleurs, j'habite à côté et je suis tombé du mur. Je m'appelle Follet, je suis un petit chat.

– Nous, on est des fleurs et on s'appelle Capucines.

Follet continue sa promenade. Il s'arrête devant un arbre immense couvert de fruits rouges.

– Bonjour, tu es aussi une fleur ?

– Une fleur ? **Ah ! Ah !**... Mais non, je suis un arbre et je m'appelle « Pommier ».

« Que de nouvelles choses ! », se dit Follet.

Follet arrive près d'un étang rempli de poissons rouges.
Un petit poisson sort la tête de l'eau et lui murmure :

– Tu es nouveau dans le jardin ?

– Oui, je viens d'arriver, lui répond Follet.

Plouf ! Le poisson plonge dans l'eau sans rien dire.

« **Oh !** Voici un drôle de chat », se dit Follet.
Il s'approche tout doucement de l'étrange animal
qui se réveille.

– Qu'est-ce que tu es toi ? Moi, je suis le petit chat Follet.

– Tu ne vois donc pas que je suis un chien ?

Et je m'appelle Puick.

– Ne te fâche pas, s'il te plaît.
Je ne connais pas encore beaucoup de choses.
Si tu veux, on peut se promener ensemble.
– D'accord, répond Puick, ravi.

Hihi ! Follet s'amuse comme un petit fou
en voyant la queue de Puick se balancer.
– C'est pour montrer que je suis content.
Regarde, dit Puick, en agitant
sa queue dans tous les sens pour faire rire son ami.

À proximité de l'étang, Follet demande à son ami
le nom du petit animal rouge qui a semblé fuir à sa vue.
– C'est un poisson, répond Puick. Il vit au fond de l'eau.
Il ne faut pas lui faire de mal,
sinon l'étang sera tout triste.

Voilà Reinette-la-grenouille
qui vient saluer Follet et Puick.
– Comme elle saute haut ! s'exclame Follet
ravi du spectacle.
– **Bravo, Bravo,** s'écrient Puick et Follet.

Ils arrivent au fond du jardin.
Puick présente Pointu-le-hérisson au petit chat.
Mais Pointu le met doucement en garde:
– **Attention,** je pique !

– Aucun ennemi ne peut m'approcher
quand je ferme mon manteau piquant !
déclare Pointu en faisant une démonstration.
– Très impressionnant, admire Follet.
J'espère que nous serons toujours amis.

– Certainement, répond Pointu tout content.
Mais il est bientôt temps de rentrer.
Comment remonter sur le mur ?

– Pas de problème, dit Puick.
Nous allons demander au grand chêne de t'aider.
– **Bien sûr**, répond le chêne de sa voix profonde.
Grimpe sur mon large tronc
et de là sur ma grosse branche.

– **Au revoir ! À bientôt !**
crient tous les nouveaux amis de Follet.
Le chêne s'étire en direction du mur.
Follet se retourne et regarde une dernière fois le jardin.
« Quelle magnifique journée ! », pense le petit chat.

Martine un personnage créés par Gilbert Delahaye et Marcel Marlier / Léaucour Création.

http://www.casterman.com

D'après « Follet le petit chat » Lucienne Erville.
Achevé d'mprimer en juillet 2010 en France par PPO. Dépôt légal : janvier 2010 ; D. 2010/0053/4.
Déposé au ministère de la Justice, Paris (loi n° 49.956 du 16 juillet 1949 sur les publications destinées à la jeunesse).
ISBN 978-2-203-02895-1